Korean Spirit and Culture Website

www.koreanhero.net

www.kscpp.net

All booklets published in the series are available on our website, as well as additional materials covering various aspects of Korean history and culture.

Published so far:

Admiral Yi Sun-sin

King Sejong the Great

Chung Hyo Ye

Fifty Wonders of Korea

Taste of Korea (Cookbook)

Online video library includes:

Temple Stay

Hanbok, the Clothes of Nature

Traditional Dance and Music

UNESCO World Heritage in Korea

Korean Economy: LG, Samsung and Hyundai

And more…

Comments from Readers

"I would like to commend you on an excellent commentary about a native son of Korea who gave his mind, body, and soul to the goal of achieving freedom for his people and his country. To say that I was mildly surprised about the incredible life and history of Admiral Yi Sun-sin is an understatement. This incredible warrior and humble person is to be greatly admired."

- Colonel Thomas Brenner (RET), USA

"Yi's patriotism was one that inspired him to do good, so pure and untouched by hate, and not like modern-day patriotism which seems to breed prejudice, arrogance and division. The way he yearned to serve his country to best of his ability was much like the way holymen serve God-- unconditionally and without attachment to results or retreat in the face of defeat. His story is an inspiration for the times we face today. In a world where leaders' motives are suspect and full of self-interest we are left hoping for leaders like Yi Sun-sin to arise."

- April Cantor, USA

"On the day before the Battle of Myongnyang, Yi Sun-sin said, 'He who seeks death will live, and he who seeks life will die.' His words charged the soldiers' spirits and changed the fate of his nation."

- Silvia Riedle, Germany

Admiral Yi Sun-sin

A brief overview of his life and achievements

He who seeks death will live, and he who seeks life will die.

© 2008 Diamond Sutra Recitation Group

Admiral Yi Sun-sin : A brief overview of his life and achievements

Published by Korean Spirit & Culture Promotion Project
www.kscpp.net

Printed and Bound by Samjung Munhwasa
Chungjeong-ro 37-18, Seodaemun-gu, Seoul

First Print 2005
Fifth Print 2009

ISBN: 0-9779613-1-1

Note on Romanization

The Romanization of Korean words in this book follows the
McCune-Reischauer system, except in the case of prominent figures
and place names for which alternative usages are better known.

Note on Names

In Korean, a surname comes before the given name.
Korean names in this book follow this convention.

Contents

I. Yi Sun-sin: A National Hero of Korea

In Korean history, which spans over five millennia, there have been many national heroes, but none compares to Yi Sun-sin who saved Choson Korea from the brink of collapse during the Japanese invasion of 1592. He is still held in high esteem by the Korean people today. In a nationwide survey conducted by Soonchunhyang University in April 2005, Yi Sun-sin was chosen as the greatest figure in Korean history by 43.8% of the vote (The Chosun Daily, April 15, 2005).

It is, therefore, regrettable that Yi Sun-sin's noble life and the marvelous deeds he performed for his country and people are not well-known outside of Korea. Admiral Yi achieved a battle record that no one in history has ever matched. Genghis Khan lost two battles out of the twenty that he fought, Napoleon Bonaparte lost four battles out of twenty three, Emperor Frederick lost four battles out of twelve, and Hannibal lost one battle out of five. In all of his twenty three battles, Admiral Yi was never once defeated. Overcoming formidable odds in terms of the number of enemy ships and troops, he led his navy to victory in every engagement he fought during seven years of war with the Japanese.

In his book, *The Influence of Sea on the Political History of Japan*, George Alexander Ballard (1862-1948), a vice-admiral of the British Royal Navy, summarized Yi's life and victories as follows.

> It is always difficult for Englishmen to admit that Nelson ever had an equal in his profession, but if any man is entitled to be so regarded, it should be this great naval commander of Asiatic race who never knew defeat and died in the presence of the enemy; of whose movements a track-chart might be compiled from the wrecks of hundreds of Japanese ships lying with their valiant crews at the bottom of the sea, off the coasts of the Korean peninsula...and it seems, in truth, no exaggeration to assert that from first to last he never made a mistake, for his work was so complete under each variety of circumstances as to defy criticism... His whole career might be summarized by saying that, although he had no lessons from past history to serve as a guide, he waged war on the sea as it should be waged if it is to produce definite results, and ended by making the supreme sacrifice of a defender of his country. (p. 66–67)

The following is an extract from a paper published by the Japanese Institute of Korean Studies.

> Togo returned from the victorious Battle of Tsushima(1905) in which he had defeated the Russian Baltic Fleet, at that time the world's most powerful naval force. He had been instated as Admiral of the Japanese Navy, and at a celebratory gathering, a member of the company exclaimed, "Your great victory is so remarkable that it deserves an everlasting place in history. You can

be regarded the equal of Admiral Nelson, who defeated Napoleon in the Battle of Trafalgar; you are indeed a god of war." To this Admiral Togo replied "I appreciate your compliment. But,…if there ever were an Admiral worthy of the name of 'god of war,' that one is Yi Sun-sin. Next to him, I am little more than a petty officer."

—Andohi, Kotaro. *History and Theory of Relations of Japan, Korea and China*, Japanese Institute of Korean Studies, 1964.

Japanese scholar Hujizka Akinao mentions in his essay "In Admiration of Admiral Yi Sun-sin" (*Kyung Hee* Vol. 8. 1977) that Togo regarded Yi as his master, and held a ceremony for him before the Battle of Tsushima (it is a Japanese custom to hold a ceremony for ancestors or historically significant figures before important occasions).

Few of the world's great war heroes have been able to avoid criticism and censure, least of all from those they fought against, enduring such taunts as 'brutal oppressors' or 'starving wolves.' Admiral Yi, in contrast, has been held as an object of admiration and reverence even among the Japanese, whose minds were swayed by his pure and absolute loyalty to his country and people, his brilliant use of strategy and tactics which led invariably to victory, his invincible courage that overcame every adverse circumstance, and his unbending integrity. This admiration is apparent in many speeches and writings by Japanese military officers and historians which speak of Admiral Yi. The following are some examples.

Throughout history there have been few generals accomplished at the tactics of frontal attack, sudden attack, concentration, and dilation. Napoleon, who mastered the art of conquering the part with the whole, can be held to have been such a general, and among admirals, two further tactical geniuses may be named: in the East,

Yi Sun-sin of Korea, and in the West, Horatio Nelson of England. Undoubtedly, Yi is a supreme naval commander even on the basis of the limited literature of the Imjin War, and despite the fact that his bravery and brilliance are not known to the West, since he had the misfortune to be born in Choson Korea. Anyone who can be compared to Yi should be better than Michiel de Ruyter from Netherlands. Nelson is behind Yi in terms of character and integrity. Yi was the inventor of the iron-clad warship known as the Turtle Ship (*Kobukson*). He was a truly great commander and a master of the naval tactics of three hundred years ago.

—Sato Destaro (1866-1942), a vice-admiral of the Japanese Navy,
A Military History of the Emperor (帝國國防史論), p. 399.

Yi Sun-sin is a famous Korean admiral who defeated the Japanese in every one of the battles at sea when Toyotomi Hideyoshi's troops invaded Choson Korea. He was unique among Choson civil and military officers for his honesty and incorruptibility, and in terms of leadership and tactics, as well as loyalty and courage, he was an ideal commander almost like a miracle. He was a renowned admiral before the time of Nelson, and has never yet had an equal in world history. Although the existence of this figure grew to be almost forgotten in Korea, the admiration of his memory was handed down in Japan through generations so that his tactics and accomplishments were researched and subjected to close study when the Japanese Navy was established during the Meiji period.

—Siba Ryotaro, "Clouds over the hill", *Sankei Newspaper*,
March 27, 1972.

Of Admiral Yi's twenty-three sea battles, the most crucial were the Battle of Hansando and the Battle of Myongnyang. In the Battle of Hansando, considered one of the greatest naval engagements in history, Yi, by means of his famous 'Crane Wing' formation, achieved a great victory by sinking and capturing fifty nine of the seventy three Japanese ships which opposed him, thereby frustrating Hideyoshi's plan of advancing along the coast. The Battle of Myongnyang, in which he defeated 130 enemy ships with only 13 ships his own, is regarded among maritime historians as nothing less than a miracle.

Yi is often compared with Admiral Nelson and Admiral Togo. All three men were heroes who fought for the destiny of their countries and saved their countrymen from foreign invasion by securing key naval victories. However, the circumstances of Nelson's Battle at Trafalgar and of Togo's Battle at Tsushima differ strikingly from those of the Battle of Myongnyang fought by Admiral Yi.

At the Battle of Trafalgar, England, a nation traditionally strong on the sea, was facing an enemy who was at that time inexperienced in naval warfare, and who commanded a fleet not much larger than her own (27 English ships against 33 French and Spanish ships). In the case of the Battle of Tsushima, the Japanese navy also had the upper hand in many respects. The Russian crews of the Baltic fleet who opposed them were exhausted after a seven-month voyage which had taken them halfway round the world; the Arctic-born Russian crews had suffered greatly from outbreaks of disease as they sailed through the equator area. Taking this into account, it is of little surprise that an intensively trained Japanese Navy, in high morale and fighting near the mainland of Japan, emerged victorious over the dispirited Russian forces. The battles discussed above may be summarized in a chart as follows:

Naval Battles of Togo, Nelson, and Yi

	Home Forces	Enemy Forces	Outcome
Togo, Heihachiro Battle of Tsushima May 27-28, 1905	4 warships 27 cruisers Other vessels (Japan)	11 warships 8 cruisers Other vessels (Russia)	Japanese Victory 25 enemy ships sunk and captured
Nelson, Horatio Battle of Trafalgar October 21, 1805	27 (England)	33 (France & Spain)	English Victory 23 enemy ships sunk and captured
Yi, Sun-sin Battle of Myongnyang September 16, 1597	13 (Korea)	130 (Japan)	Korean Victory 31 enemy ships sunk 90 enemy ships severely damaged

Admiral Yi achieved a truly legendary naval record. His greatness, however, lies not in mere battle figures, but rather in the great and noble sacrifice which he made for his country. The Imjin War, to which he dedicated both his life and his death, was not a war driven by a politician's desire for imperial expansion, but by a pure wish to defend one's country and people against a foreign invader.

II. About Yi Sun-sin

Yi Sun-sin was born on April 28, 1545 in the aristocratic neighborhood of Konchondong, Hansung (now Seoul) as the third son of Yi Chong and his wife Pyun. Although he was of good ancestry, his family was not well off because his grandfather had been embroiled in a political purge during the reign of King Chungjong and Yi's father did not pursue a civil service job. When the economic situation worsened for his family, they moved to Asan, the country home of Yi's maternal family.

At the age of 21, he married a woman from a neighboring town and had three sons and a daughter. Like any other young man of aristocratic family, he studied Confucian classics with his brothers from an early age. He began to train in the military arts when he turned 22. Although Yi was fully aware that the literary tradition was more highly regarded than the military tradition in his society, he chose the military service because of his personal convictions. But the refined writings in his dairy, reports, and poems demonstrate that he had remarkable literary talent, as well as the valor and brilliance of a warrior.

In 1572, when he was 28, Yi took a military service examination. During the exam, he fell from horseback and broke his left leg. The crowd was

astonished when they saw him quietly get up on one leg to bind the broken leg with a branch from a nearby willow tree. Four years after his first trial, at the age of 32, he passed the military service examination.

Thereafter, he was always true to his duties as a military officer while stationed at various locations. However, because of his unwillingness to compromise his integrity, he did not seek favors from those in power. As a result, Yi's military career languished and his accomplishments went unnoticed. He was even relieved of his post for refusing to participate in unlawful activities solicited by his superior. Also, he experienced a harsh demotion to a common foot soldier as a result of false accusations by another officer who blamed Yi for his own mistake.

Just a few months before the outbreak of war, he received an exceptional promotion and became the Commander of Cholla Left Naval Station. This was a result of the vigorous recommendation from Prime Minister Yu, who had known Yi since childhood and firmly believed that Choson Korea was in need of his abilities.

As soon as he became a naval commander, he took up the task of reviving and restoring the Korean Naval Force. He reorganized the administrative system, improved the condition of weapons and tightened sailors' discipline even though it was not yet clear that war was imminent. He also put his efforts in making warships and completed building a Turtle Ship just a day before the Japanese invasion. In the following seven years, Yi saved his homeland and his people by leading all his 23 naval engagements to victory with his unshakable loyalty, brilliant tactics, and indomitable spirit that transcended life and death.

While he accomplished unbelievable feats at sea as an admiral, Yi suffered continuous tragedies and hardships in his personal life, which makes his noble life even more remarkable. Even when he was faced with a King who tried to kill him, his loyalty to his country never wavered. He did not harbor a grudge against Won Kyun and his enemies at the king's court for falsely accusing him of treason. Even when the Korean Navy he had built with so much care was obliterated by Won Kyun's disastrous defeat against the Japanese Navy, he did not allow his anger and resentment to stop him from carrying out his duties. His absolute loyalty to his country and people enabled him to achieve a maritime miracle of uninterrupted victories. In 1598, at the age of 54, he died gloriously in his final battle at Noryang, which concluded the Imjin War. He was posthumously titled Chung Mu Gong (Master of Loyal Valor).

III. Historical Background

The closing years of the sixteenth century found Choson Korea beset with considerable political and economical difficulties. Incessant conflicts between political parties had led to corruption, which in turn had led to confusion in the tax system. The effects of inter-party wrangling had inevitably spread to regional governments, destabilizing national politics as a whole. The unjust and unreasonable appointments of officials and the poor administration which naturally followed them stirred distrust and resentment in the people. As a result, there was a decline in military discipline, and national defense was put at serious risk.

Meanwhile, across the Korea Strait, Toyotomi Hideyoshi had in the year 1590 put an end to 130 years of civil conflict by successfully unifying Japan under his rule. As he was dealing with the task of unification, he had looked for a way to dilute the power of feudal lords (daimyo) who were the most serious threat to his authority, and thereby reinforce the power of the central government. With this end in mind, he planned the invasion of neighboring countries so that he would be better able to control their internal feuding and divert the energy and attention of the daimyos abroad.

At first, he requested the Korean King to permit free passage through

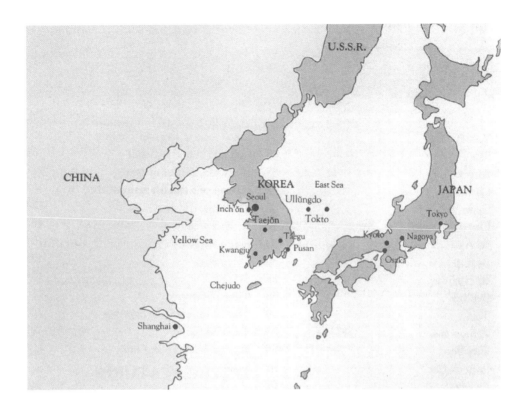

Korea for the swift movement of his army into Ming China. Korea sent a two-man mission to observe Hideyoshi's true intention and the likelihood of Japanese invasion, but they returned with conflicting opinions. Hwang expressed the possibility of invasion, while Kim thought little of the possibility. The King and the ruling classes were not alarmed. They laughed away the Japanese diplomatic approaches and ignored the possibility of war. When his overtures met with steadfast refusal, Toyotomi Hideyoshi resolved to invade the Korean peninsula.

Korea, a nation accustomed to peace for centuries, was completely unprepared when Japan presently invaded with 160,000 troops in April 1592. Against the Japanese, with their superior numbers, training, and new arms called muskets, the poorly equipped Korean military were as good as helpless. The southern defense perimeter was breached within a matter of days, and the forces of Japan began to make their way north without difficulty.

The Korean King, Sonjo, fled with his son to Pyongyang on April 30; two days later the Japanese reached the capital Seoul, eighteen days after their unopposed landing in Pusan. As the Japanese army continued their relentless advance northwards, defeating every Korean force that had the courage to face them, King Sonjo and his Court abandoned the defense of Pyongyang and fled again to Uiju, the northern tip of the Korean peninsula. The Korean people were furious with the incompetence and irresponsibility of the King and his Court. After only two months, the entire country had all but fallen to Japanese invaders.

IV. The Major Naval Battles of Yi

Fortunately, Korea had not yet lost control of the sea. Since an overland supply route would have cost too much in time and resources, the Japanese had planned to deliver supplies to their soldiers in the field by boat as the army moved northwards, making use of the southern and western coasts for landing. In this, they were disappointed; the series of naval successes that fell to the sailors of Yi Sun-sin compensated richly for the losses endured by the beleaguered Korean land forces, doing much to restore the country's tattered morale. It also greatly imperiled the situation of the Japanese soldiers by severing their lines of communication and supply, thus bringing their previously unchallenged invasion to an abrupt standstill. Following are brief accounts of the most crucial victories won in Admiral Yi's counter-campaign.

1. The Battle of Hansando and the 'Crane Wing' Formation

Admiral Yi Sun-sin, having enjoyed a continuous run of successes since May 1592, was now engaged in the task of reorganizing and restoring his naval forces at his headquarters in Yosu. Hideyoshi meanwhile was anxiously looking for an opportunity to blot out the disgrace he had incurred in recent defeats at sea. His first task was to re-establish a safe supply route. This would necessarily involve the humbling of the Korean Navy. With this in mind, he sent Wakisaka Yasuharu, one of his ablest generals, together with 70 ships and an elite detachment of his own troops to Wungchon as the First Fleet. The Second Fleet under Kuki Yoshitaka and the Third under Kato Yoshiakira later joined Wakisaka by Hideyoshi's special command.

Aware of these developments, Admiral Yi assembled a fleet of 51 ships by combining the forces of Admiral Yi Ok-ki with his own, and set off for Kyonnaeryang where Wakisaka and his fleet were riding at anchor. He was joined by Admiral Won Kyun enroute. He learned that the Kyonnaeryang channel was an unfit place for battle as it was too narrow and strewn with sunken rocks. His board-roofed ships, he reasoned, would be in danger of colliding with one another, and the nearby land would offer the enemy too near a place of refuge if they were defeated. He therefore decided to attempt to lure the enemy out into the open sea before the island of Hansando. Since Hansando lay between Koje and Kosong and was thus remote from the safety of the mainland, the Korean navy would be at liberty to attack the enemy in safety, and the enemy, if they chose to swim ashore, would face death by starvation.

According to this plan, he positioned the greater portion of his warships near Hansando and sent five or six ships into the Kyonnaeryang Channel. Seeing their meager number, the Japanese fleet set sail immediately to offer them battle. Yi then ordered the board-roofed ships to pull back as if in retreat toward Hansando, where the rest of the fleet was lying in wait. As expected, the Japanese fleet, elated by the Korean navy's feigned cowardice, redoubled their fire and began to give chase.

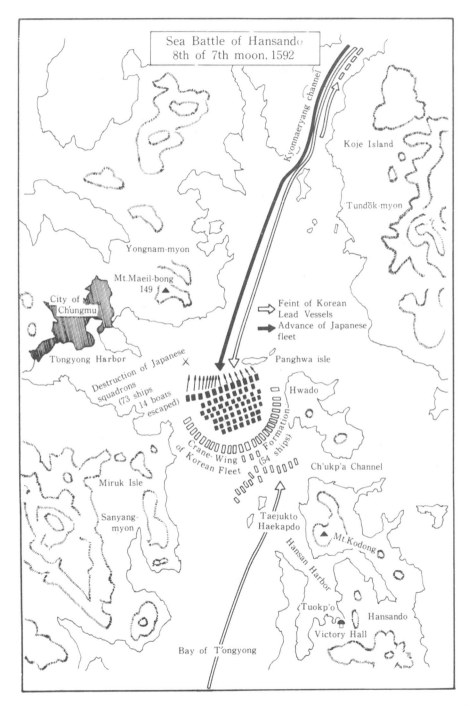

Sea Battle of Hansando
8th of 7th moon, 1592

Kyŏnnaeryang channel

Koje Island

Tundŏk-myon

Yongnam-myon

Mt.Maeil-bong
149

City of
Ch'ungmu

T'ongyong Harbor

Feint of Korean
Lead Vessels

Advance of Japanese
fleet

Panghwa isle

Destruction of Japanese
squadrons
(73 ships
14 boats
escaped)

Hwado

Crane-Wing Formation
of Korean Fleet
(54 ships)

Ch'ukp'a Channel

Miruk Isle

Sanyang-
myon

Taejukto
Haekapdo

Mt.Kodong

Hansan Harbor

Tuokp'o

Victory Hall

Hansando

Bay of T'ongyong

Yi took care to maintain a fixed distance between his own ships and those of the pursuing enemy. When they emerged into the open sea, and had reached the agreed spot near the island, he shouted suddenly,

"Now, turn and face the enemy! Turn about in Hagik-jin[1]! Attack the flagship first!"

Immediately, the Korean fleet turned to face the Japanese and spread out in Hagik-jin, surrounding the foremost vessels in a semi-circle; the Japanese, before they knew it, were trapped with little room to maneuver and had little choice but to remain where they were and weather the storm of cannon balls and fire arrows which Yi's ships now poured upon them. Seeing the fate of their comrades, the remaining enemy ships scattered and fled in all directions in great confusion and were pursued hotly by the Korean fleet. In this engagement, without any losses of their own, Admiral Yi's navy burned and sank 47 enemy ships and captured 12, leaving Wakisaka only 14 ships out of 73, a thousand men out of ten thousand.[2]

James Murdoch and Isoh Yamagata write in their book, *A History of Japan*, as follows.

---

[1] Crane Wing formation (Kor. Hagik-jin): One of Admiral Yi's famed naval formations. A Turtle-ship sails at the head of a detachment of board-roofed ships, which spread out in a curved line resembling a crane's wing when they come close to the enemy, thus surrounding him before attacking. The renowned Japanese history journal, *History Studies* (歷史研究, May 2002) revealed that Admiral Togo's 'T' formation, used in the Battle of Tsushima, was based on this formation by Admiral Yi.

[2] No conclusive evidence exists for the loss of 9000 men, but it is by no means an improbable estimate. The Japanese Navy lost 35 large-sized ships, each of which would have typically held 200 men, as well as 17 medium-sized and 7 small-sized ships which would have carried 100 and 40 men each respectively, producing a total of 8980, a figure which is supported by the account of Je Man-chun, an eye-witness of the battle who, while held as a prisoner-of-war in Japan, was able to inspect the "Official Record of the Number of Personnel Recruited and Sent Overseas" (兵糧調發件記), in which it was recorded that Wakisaka had initially 10,000 men under him but later 1,000.

It [the Battle of Hansando] may well be called Salamis of Korea. It signed the death-warrant of the invasion. It frustrated the great motive of the expedition - the humbling of China; and thenceforth, although the war dragged through many a long year, it was carried on solely with a view to mitigating the disappointment of Hideyoshi. (p. 337)

Having suffered a catastrophic loss in this last serious gamble, Toyotomi Hideyoshi forbade sea battles to be fought against the Korean Navy from then on. The Battle of Hansando, apart from being one of the three most glorious Korean victories in the Imjin War—the other two being those won at Chinju and Haengju, both land battles—is also considered as ranking among the greatest naval battles of world history.

George Alexander Ballard (1862–1948), a vice-admiral of the British Royal Navy, paid the following tribute to Admiral Yi's extraordinary achievements leading up to the Battle of Hansando in his book, *The Influence of the Sea on the Political History of Japan.*

This [the Battle of Hansando] was the great Korea admiral's crowning exploit. In the short space of six weeks he had achieved a series of successes unsurpassed in the whole annals of maritime war, destroying the enemy's battle fleets, cutting his lines of communication, sweeping up his convoys,...and bringing his ambitious schemes to utter ruin. Not even Nelson, Blake, or Jean Bart could have done more than this scarcely known representative of a small and cruelly oppressed nation; and it is to be regretted that his memory lingers nowhere outside his native land, for no impartial judge could deny him the right to be accounted among the born leaders of men. (p. 57)

The effects of Yi's latest victory were considerable. The Koreans were now the undisputed masters of the sea, and the Japanese on the Korean mainland were completely isolated from their country's support. Shortly after the battle, Pyongyang was returned to Korean hands, with the aid of the Ming Chinese forces who had arrived to relieve the land army. Two months later Seoul was abandoned by the invaders, who were compelled to submit to a truce agreement. In recognition of his ample role in bringing about this happy outcome, Yi was instated as Tongjesa and given the command of the combined naval forces of three provinces, which was then the highest honour in the Korean Navy.

2. The Battle of Myongnyang, A Maritime Miracle

In December 1596, when negotiations between Ming China and Japan had broken down, Hideyoshi renewed his Korean invasion plans after a standstill of four years. Meanwhile, Admiral Yi was having trouble due to an accusation laid against him by General Won Kyun and the intrigues of the Japanese double-agent Yoshira. Won Kyun, who had always resented that Yi should hold a position higher than his own, had not only deliberately countermanded many of Yi's orders in the past, but also frequently made false reports to the King's Court concerning the state of the navy and the results of battles so as to defame Yi's character. As a result, there was a growing suspicion at court that the flourishing admiral could not be trusted.

The Japanese were aware that if they were to succeed in their fresh invasion plans, they would need first to eliminate the man who had been the ruin of all their former attempts. To that end, they devised a plan to oust him from the favor of the King.

A Japanese soldier named Yoshira was sent to the camp of the Korean general, Kim Eung-su, where he offered to work for the Koreans as a spy. The general readily agreed, and Yoshira was able to act the role of an informer, giving the Koreans what appeared to be valuable information. One day he reported to General Kim as follows: 'Before long, General Kato Kiyomasa of Japan will arrive in Korea. I will soon be able to provide you with full details regarding the exact time and the ship on which he is sailing, but in the meantime, let Korea send the Tongjesa to intercept him.'

General Kim believed him and sought permission from King Sonjo to send Admiral Yi to the scene of the enemy's expected approach. The King granted the request and ordered Yi to dispatch his ships. Yi, however, found himself unable to obey the King's order because he knew that the given location was highly dangerous with many submerged rocks. It would have been an act of suicide to attempt any kind of naval operation in such conditions. When informed of this by General Kim, King Sonjo was greatly angered, assuming that Yi was disobeying him out of haughtiness. Yi was placed under arrest and taken to Seoul in chains, where he was beaten and tortured. The King wanted to have him put to death, but Yi's supporters at Court convinced him to spare the admiral in view of his many past services to the throne. Spared the death penalty, the Tongjesa was demoted to the rank of common foot soldier, a humiliation he accepted without a word of complaint or resentment.

Won Kyun, thanks to the exertions of his partisans, the Soin faction at court, was instated as Tongjesa in Yi Sun-sin's place, as he had wished for so long. He was, however, far inferior to Yi in his direction of naval affairs and lazy in the duties of managing the sailors and the fleet. Meanwhile, the spy Yoshira continued to urge General Kim to send the Korean Navy to intercept the fleet of Japanese ships, which he announced were now on the point of arriving. The order was given, and Won Kyun, having marshaled together every ship he could find, reluctantly set sail.

The result, as might have been predicted, was disastrous and made even worse by Won Kyun's inept and clumsy maneuvers, by which he very narrowly avoided bringing the entire Korean fleet to destruction. Panic-stricken and having lost the confidence of all his men, the admiral fled to land, only to be beheaded by a Japanese soldier lying in wait for him. This battle was the sole naval defeat experienced by the Korean Navy throughout the whole course of the Imjin War, but its outcome was devastating and irreparable. Of the Korean Navy's 134 warships, a mere 12 escaped to safety under Commander Pae Sol.

Upon hearing the news of Won Kyun's disastrous defeat, the King repented his rash decision and hastily reinstated Yi as Supreme Naval Commander. Yi Sun-sin, in spite of his previous shameful demotion and the recent heartbreaking news of his mother's death, made his way to headquarters, ready to do his duty. During the journey, he planned his campaign. He ventured to take the longer, more dangerous route around the Cholla Province in the face of his pursuing enemies, so that he would be able to gather together the remaining ships with the help of refugees, requisition supplies and weapons, and enlist new recruits. He visited the officials of each village he passed through in order to give them encouragement and to help restore the collapsed local administration. He nursed within himself a passionate sense of duty and a loyal conviction that the destiny of his country and people now depended on his labors.

When he arrived, he found that he had only 12 ships at his disposal. He managed to obtain one more ship, provided by local residents. The King's Court, learning of the pitiful condition of the fleet, urged Yi to give up the fight at sea and to join his forces with those of the land army, which would mean the effective dissolution of the Korean Navy. Yi, however, submitted the following memorial to the throne insisting on the importance of preserving the country's naval force.

> During the past five or six years, since the earliest days of the war, the enemy have been unable to penetrate the Chungchong and Cholla provinces directly, for our navy has blocked their way. Your humble servant still commands no fewer than twelve ships. If I engage the enemy fleet with resolute effort, even now, as I believe, they can be driven back. The total decommissioning of our navy would not only please the enemy, but would open up for him the sea route along the coast of Chungchong Province, enabling him to sail up the Han River itself, which is my heart's greatest fear. Even though our navy is small, I promise you that as long as I live, the enemy cannot despise us.
>
> — *A Complete Collection on Chung Mu Gong Yi, Vol. 9*

Yi's memorial convinced the King and his courtiers, and the plans to abandon the navy were set aside. Meanwhile, despite his seemingly hopeless situation, Yi was doing his best to prepare for the coming battle. To cope with the enemy's vastly greater numbers, the engagement would have to take place in a long narrow strait through which the enemy fleet would only be able to enter by dividing into smaller groups. On the southern coast, there were only two places befitting this description: Kyonnaeryang and Myongnyang. The former was already under Japanese control, and so Yi moved his headquarters to Myongyang with all speed.

Myongnyang was a passageway the Japanese had to go through to attack Seoul (capital city), as they advanced from the South to the West Sea, and up the Han River. As the waters of the expansive sea are forced into its narrow strait, the drift of the current noticeably increases; at its fastest, it reaches 10 knots (approximately 18 km/h), strongest of all the channels in the Korean peninsula. And beneath the narrow and fast waterway of Myongnyang, Yi mapped out a plan to lay a massive underwater trap in the form of an iron rope tied to a capstan, a blockade device that would catch the Japanese ships, and cause them to capsize and collide with each other amidst the strong, fast current. The mainstay of the Korean war vessels at the time were designed with a U-shaped base that was shallow and flat, but the Japanese Navy had a V-shaped hull which was deep and sharp. An underwater obstacle, therefore, was an effective way to stop the Japanese Navy.

On September 15, 1597, one day before the decisive battle, Admiral Yi called together all his staff officers and ships' captains and delivered the following address:

> "According to the principles of strategy, 'He who seeks death will live, and he who seeks life will die.' And again, 'If one defender stands watch by a strong gateway, he may drive terror deep into the heart of an enemy coming up by the ten thousand.' To men in our condition, these sayings are worth more than gold. You, my Captains, are expected to render strict obedience to my commands. If you do not, not even the least error will be pardoned, nay, but severely punished according to Martial Law".
>
> —*War Diary*, September 15, 1597

Early in the morning, on the 16th of September, Yi received news that a large fleet of Japanese ships was approaching his base. He called on all of his captains to take the Oath of Valor. Then he weighed anchor and put out to sea at the head of his fleet, ready to engage an enemy fleet of 330 war vessels with only 13 of his own.

The thirteen ships of the Korean Navy stood arrayed against the enemy in Ilja-jin (One Line Formation). Ilja-jin is one of the simplest formations, consisting of a group of ships lined abreast with their prows facing the enemy; understandably, with only 13 ships, Yi was not at liberty to attempt anything more complex or diverse. Thus a single battle line of the Korean Navy faced a huge enemy fleet of over 300 vessels.

Owing to the narrowness of the channel, only 130 Japanese ships were able to come in to attack, and before long, they had surrounded Admiral Yi's fleet. Outnumbered by ten to one, the overwhelmed captains of the Korean Navy stealthily began to pull back in fear. Yi's flagship sped forward alone into the midst of the advancing enemy, fearlessly bombarding them with a constant volley of arrows and gunfire.

As the Japanese fleet enveloped the flagship with line after line, the sailors on board lost heart and crouched down, motionless. Admiral Yi quietly remonstrated with them, "Though the enemy may boast of his thousand warships, he will not dare come near us. Have no fear! Engage the enemy with all your might!" Yi looked about for his other ships, but they had already fallen astern from the flagship by some distance.

He raised the military command flag and hoisted a call signal towards the captains, whereupon they drew nearer to the flagship. Admiral Yi called to one of them furiously, "Do you want to be hanged under court martial? Do you want to die by military command? Do you think you can live by hanging back?" Awakened by these words, the ships of An and Kim charged the enemy line at full speed, and fought desperately. But they soon grew exhausted in the face of the countless enemies who crowded in unceasingly against them.

At that moment, the tide of the battle was turned by a single fortunate circumstance. On Admiral Yi's flagship there was a Japanese defector who worked for Yi as a translator. As he looked down upon the enemy soldiers

Sea Battle of Myongnyang
16th of 9th moon, 1597

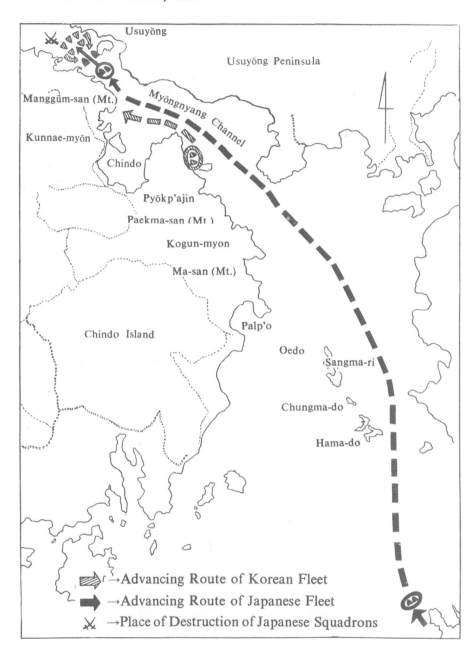

Usuyŏng

Usuyŏng Peninsula

Myŏngnyang Channel

Manggŭm-san (Mt.)

Kunnae-myŏn

Chindo

Pyŏkp'ajin

Paekma-san (Mt.)

Kogun-myon

Ma-san (Mt.)

Chindo Island

Palp'o

Oedo

Sangma-ri

Chungma-do

Hama-do

→Advancing Route of Korean Fleet

→Advancing Route of Japanese Fleet

→Place of Destruction of Japanese Squadrons

and sailors swimming in blood on the surface of the sea, the dead body of a man clothed in a red brocade uniform caught his eye; it was Matashi, the Japanese general. Straightaway, Admiral Yi ordered his men to haul up the floating body and display it to the enemy, suspending it from the top of the mast. As expected, the sight of their dead commander sent terror and dread sweeping through the Japanese navy.

Just then, the current of the Myongnyang, which changes direction four times a day, every six hours, turned against the Japanese Navy, in favor of the Korean fleet, putting the formations of both sides out of order. Admiral Yi quickly took command and at his encouragement the Korean ships darted forward beating drums and calling out battle cries. The Japanese fleet scattered and took flight. Taking advantage of the tide's new direction, the confined nature of the battleground, and the cumbersome size of the enemy fleet, now a weakness rather than strength, Yi's fleet drove the enemy into a melee of chaos and destruction.

The capstan turned, the iron ropes tightened. As their front edges and the rudders entangled with the iron ropes, the Japanese ships rushing in retreat capsized into the strong current and collided into each other. It was a scene of turmoil.

As they lost order, the Japanese ships became entangled, ramming into one another, as if fighting amongst themselves. The Korean Navy meanwhile kept up the attack, hailing down arrows and firing the cannons marked "Earth" and "Black" (For an explanation of these terms, see section V on the Kobukson). Of the 130 enemy warcraft that entered the Myongnyang Channel, 31 ships were sunk and more than 90 were severely damaged; none of the Korean ships were lost. Such was the Battle of Myongnyang, won, as Admiral Yi wrote in his diary, purely by the grace of heaven, and regarded as a miracle in the history of marine warfare.

3. The Battle of Noryang, The Final Battle

Japan's second invasion of Korea in 1597 was encumbered once again by the formidable presence of Admiral Yi on the sea as well as the volunteer Korean patriots and Chinese relief forces on land. The death of Hideyoshi in August of the following year brought with it the recall of the Japanese forces from Korea. Admiral Yi decided to block the enemy's return route in collaboration with the Ming Chinese Navy, at that time under the command of Admiral Chen Lien.

Chen Lien, however, had been offered a bribe by Konish Yukinaga, a Japanese general, in return for his granting the Japanese Navy a safe passage back to Japan. The two admirals, therefore, with opposite purposes, each attempted to persuade the other, the one hoping to destroy the retreating Japanese force, the other to spare it. In the end, Lien could do nothing but accept Yi's adamant intention to intercept the fleeing enemy forces. While these plans were being made, Yukinaga sent a message to his colleague Simath Yoshihiro and requested him to assemble the entire Japanese fleet at Noryang, planning to make one final attack on the combined naval forces of Korea and China during their retreat.

Yi therefore ordered his crews to sail out to Noryang, where he engaged the Japanese in a fierce battle, in which 50 enemy ships were destroyed. Around daybreak the following day, the Japanese Navy, unable to resist any longer, began to flee towards Kwaneumpo, imagining that they were heading for open sea. Upon reaching it, however, they discovered that they were blocked in on every side. Left with no choice but to turn back and fight, the Japanese ships charged at the flagship of Admiral Yi. Chen Lien, discovering that Yi was in trouble, penetrated the encircling line of the enemy fleet and brought him to safety. As the battle continued, however, it was now Chen Lien who found himself surrounded by a circle of enemy ships. Yi, noticing three enemy generals standing in the bow of the Main Command ship directing and encouraging their fleet, ordered all his gunners to aim at them. Of the three, one was killed. The noose then loosened as the encircling ships headed towards their Main Command ship for her protection, and Chen Lien was safe.

The combined Korean and Chinese navies then renewed their attack on the Japanese, sinking 200 of their ships. As Admiral Yi, roaring out the call to advance, led the fleet in a final foray against the forces that remained, he was hit by a stray bullet from an enemy vessel and fell mortally wounded. Yi bid his men cover him with a shield. "The battle is at its height," he said to them, "Tell no one of my death." These final words he left behind him as a bequest of loyalty to his country. By his side stood his eldest son Hoe and his nephew Wan with bows in their hands. Holding back their tears, they continued to wave the flag and beat the drum, signaling to the navy to fight on.

Admiral Yi's sailors did not slacken in their efforts until the very last moments of the battle were over. As a result, only 50 out of the 500 Japanese were able to escape. It was this, the Battle of Noryang, which finally put an end to the Imjin War.

V. The Kobukson or 'Turtle Ship'

The Kobukson, also known as the Turtle Ship, was the first ironclad warship in the world. Boasting unparalleled firepower and mobility, it proved a pivotal instrument for victory in the sea battles under Admiral Yi. Effectively a sea tank, it was capable of sinking large numbers of enemy vessels and did much to maintain the morale of Korean sailors.

It should not be supposed that Admiral Yi designed and built the Turtle Ship entirely by himself. The planning and the actual construction of the Kobukson required the combined efforts of a large number of people, both craftsmen and naval officers. On the practical side of the work, for instance, Na Tae-yong (1556~1612) played one of the most important roles in bringing the plans for the ship to fruition.

An Overview of Kobukson

The following are the main features of Kobukson, as recorded by Yi Sun-sin's nephew, Yi Pun, in his book, *Haeng Rok*.

Replica of Kobukson at the War Memorial of Korea

1. Its dimensions are 34.2m in length, 6.4m in height, and 10.3m in width; it is thus roughly the same size as a Panokson (the standard warship of the Korean Navy at the time of the Imjin War).
2. The prow is fashioned in the shape of a dragon's head; cannon balls are fired through the mouth.
3. The stern is in the shape of a turtle's tail. Additional gun ports are stationed beneath it.
4. The turtle's 'back' is a roof made with planks and is covered with iron spikes. Amid the spikes is a narrow, cross-shaped alley that serves as a passageway along the roof for the crew to use.
5. Six gun ports are positioned on each side of the deck.
6. During combat the spikes on the roof are concealed with straw mats, on which an unsuspecting enemy will be impaled if he tries to board.
7. Any attack from port or starboard is repelled by arrows and cannon fire,

which can be launched from every part of the ship.

8. From the inside, the outside can be seen, but the inside cannot be seen from the outside.

9. It employs every variety of projectile-based weapon, including long-ranging cannons such as Chon (Heaven), Chi (Earth), Hyon (Black) and Hwang (Yellow).

10. As such, it is able to roam freely and unopposed amid many hundreds of enemy ships.

Detailed Description of Kobukson

The Kobukson was mounted with a dragon's head at the bow and a turtle's tail at the stern. It had two decks; a lower deck for oarsmen and an upper deck for archers and gunners. It was specially designed so that its sailors could see their enemies outside while remaining invisible.

In the naval warfare of the day, it was usual to attempt to board an opponent's ship and engage him in hand-to-hand combat. The Kobukson was designed to make this kind of assault particularly difficult. Not only was the ship roofed over, protecting both combat (45) and non-combat (80) personnel alike, but the roof itself was fitted with deadly iron spikes, which were often concealed beneath innocent-looking straw mats.

Unlike other warships, the Kobukson had guns stationed not only along its sides, but also in the bow and in the stern, allowing it unprecedented accuracy and flexibility of range in firepower. The dragon head was designed not only to 'breathe out' flaming arrows and cannon balls, but also sulfurous fumes and clouds of smoke, which provided the Korean Navy with cover for tactical maneuvers, as well as frightening the more superstitious of the Japanese sailors.

A little below the bow, there protruded the head of a gargoyle, which served as a charging device, and together with the dragon head constituted the secret of the Kobukson's tactic of ramming. In battle, the Kobukson would charge an enemy ship and, once the gargoyle's head had breached its hull, cannon balls would be fired from the dragon's head into the breach as the ship withdrew. The gargoyle had the further effect of improving the ship's hydrodynamic performance by cutting the waves as the ship sped along, thus increasing its ramming speed.

Two further features of the Kobukson made it particularly serviceable for the execution of this tactic. First, it was built with Red Pine timbers no less than 12cm in diameter; the advantage offered by this type of wood was that its relative density of 0.73 was much higher than that of average timber, which lay typically between 0.41-0.47. Second, wooden nails were used in the construction of the Kobukson. Unlike metal, which was quick to rust, the wooden nails absorbed water and expanded, and thus over time the joints became more secure. The Kobukson as a whole was constructed on this principle: support beams were fitted to the roofs by means of a system of matching indentations and interlocking teeth, thus making the entire structure of the vessel stronger and more resilient.

The Japanese ships, built out of wood with a low density, were light and swift, but the relative weakness of the wood to withstand the recoil of cannon put a restriction on the number of heavy fire-arms that could be carried on one ship. Consequently they normally preferred to use muskets, which had a maximum range of 200 meters. The Kobukson, on the other hand, were able to carry a whole array of different cannons on board, including long-distance cannons such as the Chon (Heaven) with a range of over 500 meters, the Chi (Earth), its slightly smaller companion, which had a range of 350 meters, and the Sung (Victory), a portable cannon with a range of up to 200 meters.

Kobukson had eight oars on either side, with a team of five men — a leader and four regular oarsmen — assigned to each oar, making a total rowing crew of 80. During combat every oarsman was expected to be on duty, but at other times they would take turns at the oar in pairs. The leader would direct his colleagues to row forward or backward, to increase or decrease speed, to halt or turn about, according to the changing circumstances of the battle. This innovative division of duties thus gave the Kobukson superior potential of movement not only in terms of speed but also in terms of the range of its possible maneuvers.

The combat personnel on board the Kobukson were divided into three groups: gunners, chargers responsible for the loading of cannons with shells and gunpowder, and archers. It was thus possible for the Kobukson to produce an uninterrupted shower of cannon balls and fire-arrows, wreaking havoc on everything that came within its range.

The number of gun ports generally varied from ship to ship, but the Tongjeyong Kobukson which we find described in *The Complete Works of Yi Sun-sin* had a total of 74: 12 ports on either side of the turtle's back, 44 on either side of the shielded boards underneath, 2 above and below dragon's head, and so on.

Invented late in the 16th century, Kobukson was a unique warship, the like of which cannot be found used anywhere else in world naval history. Planned with meticulous care, and the result of much detailed scientific research, it boasted unsurpassed structure and performance. Above all, much meaning lies in the fact that Kobukson was a refinement and a remodeling of the Panokson, the existing warship of Korea, based on careful investigation of the primary Japanese tactic of grappling and boarding.

Replicas of *Kobukson* are on display at various national museums, such as the War Memorial of Korea, as well as other museums in many other countries including China, Japan, Germany, France, USA, and Canada.

VI. The War Diary of Yi Sun-sin

Yi Sun-sin kept a careful record of daily events in his diary. This diary, when completed, contained some 2539 entries, both private and official, together comprising an account of his life in the camps during the period of the Imjin War. The first entry appears on January 1, 1592, the day of his appointment as Admiral of the Left Cholla Province, and the last on November 17, 1598, two days before his death at the battle of Noryang. Two copies of the diary have been handed down to us: one is the original diary (designated National Treasure No.76) and is housed at the Asan Memorial Shrine, and the second is to be found in *The Complete Works of Yi Sun-sin*, a work edited and published by Yun Hang-im by Royal Command in the 19th year of King Chongjo's reign, 1795. Admiral Yi did not give an official title to his diary, but it has been known as *War Diary* (Kor. *Nangjung Ilgi*) since Yun conceived it as a convenient title when compiling his *Complete Works*.

War Diary is a source of utmost historical importance, as its detailed pages provide for us the most reliable information about the course of events during the Imjin War. Not only this, but it is from its entries that we have learned much of what we know today about the mind and

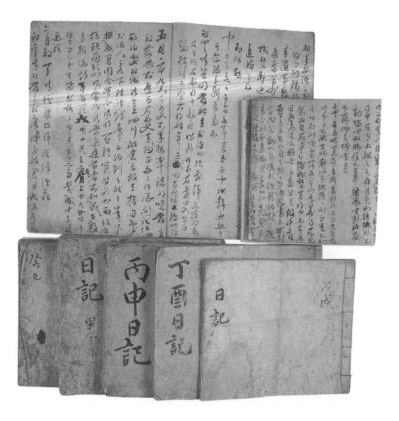

Yi Sun-sin's *War Diary*

character of a hero who lived almost half a millennium ago. *War Diary* presents a vivid description of Admiral Yi's daily life, military affairs, secret strategic meetings, of social visits from friends, family, colleagues and celebrities, of rewards and punishment, correspondence, personal reflections on the state of the country, and so on. Like a warrior's writing, the diary was written in a simple yet sincere language, and its bold brush strokes illustrate the gallant spirit of the author, making the *War Diary* a true work of art.

VII. Life and Death of Admiral Yi Sun-sin

The life and splendid accomplishments of Admiral Yi took place amid grim hardships and constant adversities; his country was in crisis and his people were suffering. From the outside he had the Japanese to contend with, from within, the jealousy and mischievous slanders of the King and his Court. The war in which he took part was a desperate fight on which the fate of his nation depended and was a heavy responsibility, one undertaken in spite of the almost total absence of material support and reinforcement from central or local governments.

The one thing Yi received from the government was the position of Tongjesa, Supreme Naval Commander, which immediately made him the target of political antagonism and intrigue, and later became the cause of his demotion and imprisonment. The local governments were officially obliged to provide the navy with supplies for battle, but the collection and distribution of these supplies were made almost impossible by the constant desertion of the land by farmers and the incorrigible venality of local officials. The results spoke for themselves. In 1593, the Korean Navy suffered from serious starvation in their camp at Hansando. Around 600 sailors (that is, around 10% of the total manpower) died of hunger, while the rest endured malnutrition and serious illness. In such circumstances, it was a hard task indeed for Admiral Yi to muster sufficient numbers of men to fight for him.

Yi's work was not limited to commanding his men in battles. He was also responsible for provisions, military supplies, distribution, recruitment, care for the wounded, shipbuilding, manufacture of cannon and ammunition, farming, and salt production as a source of raising money. In short, he had to provide for every aspect of warfare by and for himself. The government, meanwhile, so far from lending him support, would even occasionally demand that he should send supplies of paper and weapons for the Royal Court from his camp.

Yi's political misfortunes dated back to the days before his appointment in the Royal Navy when he served as a junior officer. His promising career was suddenly cut short when he became an innocent victim of the bitter struggle for power between the warring parties at court. Yi Sun-sin was a man whose only loyalties were to his country and to his principles. A man of this kind, for whom personal glory and influence held so little interest, and who never paid deference to power for its own sake, was naturally a thorn in the side of the corrupt politicians who were his contemporaries. In actuality, it was his upright character which constituted the true substance of the accusation laid against Yi Sun-sin at Hansando. Officially, however, it was charged that he had:

(1) Deceived and thereby held in contempt the throne and his court.
(2) Betrayed his country by failing to attack a retreating enemy.
(3) Assumed credit for others' accomplishments and slandered the innocent: thus showing an unreserved and impudent attitude.

These grave allegations were the fruits of Yi Sun-sin's disastrous relationship with General Won Kyun that had begun soon after the outbreak of war and also the result of the efforts of the Japanese double agent Yoshira who worked to eliminate Yi and thus clear the path for the Japanese campaign.

Seven Royal Assemblies were held in order to determine Yi's fate. The discussion held among the courtiers was recorded for us by the Sonjo Sillok (Royal Archives). From this, it is clear that King Sonjo had already decided that Yi should be killed, and that he was constantly soliciting the agreement of the court by means of subtle hints. The admiral's supporters, however, succeeded in convincing the King that the execution of a general during wartime could only be in the interests of the enemy. In this way, Yi narrowly escaped being put to death and was led back to prison. When the second Japanese invasion took place, he found himself fighting as a common foot soldier. In a rigidly hierarchical society such as the Choson Dynasty of Korea, demotion from Supreme Naval Command to the rank of common soldier was one of the worst humiliations imaginable, worse than even the death penalty.

It is a testament to the noble nature of Yi Sun-sin that in his diary we find no mention of his torture and demotion, nor of political intrigue and persecution. Neither is any trace of his misfortune and disgrace to be found in much of the literature written about him by others. He left no record or statement on the subject of his dishonor and dismissal. As a disgraced private soldier, he kept his silence; and later, when he had to fight with only 13 ships against a 130-strong enemy fleet after Won Kyun's disastrous defeat, he quietly did his duty without blaming anyone.

Yi, who had returned as the Tongjesa, had once again saved Choson Korea with his great victory at Myongnyang. At the news of the victorious battle, the entire populace, the government officials, and even the Ming generals were astounded and greatly rejoiced. Meanwhile, the Japanese, having suffered a disastrous defeat, dispatched 50 soldiers to Yi's home in Asan in revenge. They burned the house and plundered the neighborhood. Other family members narrowly escaped to mountains nearby, but his third son Myon, who remained, fought against them with a bow and a sword in his hand. Killing three Japanese soldiers, resisting till the end, he finally lost his life to the enemy's sword. He was then 21 years old. The death of his beloved son deeply scarred Yi's heart and left him in an even worse state of health.[3]

The task of leading and controlling his men was never an easy one. The crimes of robbery, rape, disobedience, mutiny, drunkenness, desertion, divulgence of military secrets, improper recruitment, espionage, dissemination of false rumors – all these took place, as they do in all such camps during wartime.

Yi Sun-sin, however, forced his men to face the hellish reality of life, the wretched plight of the Korean Navy, and never accepted any excuse for

---

[3] Yi sun sin expresses his painful sorrow over the death of his youngest son in his diary as follows: How could the Heavens be so merciless. It is as if my heart is being burned and torn to pieces. Proper, by Nature, it is I who should have died and it is you who should have lived. Yet since you are dead and I alive, how contrary to Nature, how improper is it. The heavens and the earth are dark, and even the sun has lost its color. Ah, how sad! My son, where are you now, having deserted me? Is it because you are such an outstanding figure that the heavens are unwilling to leave you in this world, or is it because of my sin, that this great misfortune has befallen you? Even if I hold out in this world, now on whom can I lean my heart? I wish to follow you to the grave, to stay and weep with you together under the ground, but if I do, your brothers, sisters and your mother will have no one to lean their hearts on. Thus I endure, but my mind that wails is already dead, soulless. Passing a night now seems like waiting for a year to go by. (*War Diary*, October 14, 1597)

"It has been exactly four days since I heard the news of my youngest son's death. I had been unable to weep freely, so I went to the house of Kang Makji, the fire-tender at the saltern, and cried." (October 16, 1597) [Editor's Note] Yi could not express his sorrow in the presence of his seamen so he had sought privacy at Kang's house.

avoiding them. He shared with his men the firm belief that 'He who seeks death will live, and he who seeks life will die.' He put his belief into practice by always leading his navy from the front in battle and was wounded in the Battle of Sachon as a result of this courageous policy.

Throughout his whole career, Yi Sun-sin fought face-to-face with death on behalf of his country and countrymen, and in the last battle of the war, he finally offered up his life.

VIII. Conclusion

Sitting alone under a lighted candle, I took thought of the present state
of our nation's affairs; I found the tears rolling down my cheeks.

—*War Diary*, January 1, 1595

At times, he agonized in tears as he watched his soldiers train while enduring starvation. He sacrificed himself and tended to the needs of his soldiers and people before his own. He carried forth his love for them.

With his uncompromising loyalty, his dauntless will, and steadfast courage, he saved his country when its leaders were lost in the crisis of war. He firmly held on to honest principles, put an end to evil customs, and led his men with thorough preparation and a pioneering spirit. He possessed unshakable conviction, achieved repeated successes in battles by means of brilliant tactics and strategy, and by his unselfish devotion, gained the absolute trust of his men. He had no experienced, well-trained navy as Admiral Togo and Admiral Nelson had, nor was he himself trained as an admiral. His country was small and weak and unable to support him.

However, even the Heavens were moved by his noble spirit of loyalty, and he attained the legendary record of 23 consecutive victories. He raised up fruit from barren earth. Indeed, he created everything from nothing.

To Koreans, he is not a hero, but a holy hero.

He is Admiral Yi Sun-sin.

Appendix

A. Admiral Yi's *War Diary* and *Memorials to Court*

B. The Warships and Weaponry of Korea and Japan

C. Pictures of Kobukson

D. The Admiralship of Yi Sun-sin

E. Yi Sun-sin: His Memories and Influence on Korea Today

F. Naval Battles of Admiral Yi

G. Chronological Career Note

Admiral Yi's War Diary and Memorials to Court

The English versions of Admiral Yi Sun-sin's *War Diary* and *Memorials to Court* have been published by Yonsei University Press. Written from the admiral's own perspective, they give a vivid description of his life at sea and the situations he faced during the war. Because these records were written by a man of strict integrity, who lived in a society where the progression of the war was reported meticulously to the king by his overseers, they provide trustworthy accounts of the events of the battles and are free from the exaggerations and inaccuracies so typical of historical records of wars. Here are a few selected entries of the diary and memorials, a clear mirror that reflects Yi's noble life and profound spirit in various aspects.

Memorials to Court: 1. Emergency Measures Against Japanese Invasion

Yi, Your Majesty's humble subject, Commander of Cholla Left Naval Station, addresses the throne about some emergency measures against the enemy attack. Today, on the 15th of fourth moon at 8:00 p.m., I received from Won Kyun, Commander of Kyongsang Right Naval Station, an official dispatch with the information that urgent reports from Commandant Chon Ung-nin of Kadok Fort and Captain Hwang Chong-nok of Ch'onsongp'o had reached him on the 14th at 10 a.m., relaying the alarms given by Yi On, the lighthouse keeper at Ungbong and So Kon, the beacon watch in Naesanmyon, Kimhae-gun, that on the 13th at 4 p.m., about ninety Japanese vessels, having passed by Chugido, sailed toward Pusanpo in a long line of battle and that the commandant ordered his right-wring captain at Tadaepo, Pusan to lead his warships out to sea to watch the movements of the Japanese vessels.

In the above dispatch Won Kyun saw these vessels as the Japanese trading boats coming to our land annually, but the continuous arrival of such a larger merchant fleet of ninety vessels is an uncommon event. In order to cope with the worst possible condition that might befall us, I sent official dispatches of warning to all ports under my command to watch carefully in full war-alert day and night, and I also stand on the watchtower at the entrance of the sea with my battleships in martial array.

I report as above for today. I must add that in another official dispatch on the same day Won Kyun stated that he had received a special dispatch at 4 p.m., from Pak Hong, Commander of Kyongsang Left Naval Station, based on an urgent report from Commandant of Kadok Fort - "One hundred and fifty Japanese vessels are entering the harbors of Haeundae and Pusan." Won Kyun expressed his grave concern, saying that these are not the Japanese trading boats on their annual visit to Korea. It will take a long time to analyze the individual items of the messages, so here I transmit their main points only and will report on the coming developments of the situation. I will maintain battle-ships at the entrance of the sea to meet any emergency that might arise. At the same time, I sent round circular letters to the Provincial Governor, the Army Commander, and the Commander of Cholla Right Naval Station in addition to the keepers of coastal towns and ports, calling upon them to be on the alert.

Yi, Commander
8:00 p.m., 15th of Fourth Moon, 1592

Memorials to Court: 9. Defeating the Japanese at Kyonnaeryang [the Hansando Battle]

I memorialize the throne about the capture and slaughter of the enemy. Before the arrival of the royal orders, the Japanese robbers, roving on the sea of Kyongsang Province, gradually encroached upon the coastal areas under the jurisdiction of the Kyongsang Right Naval Station, burning and plundering everywhere until the invaded Sach'on, Kongyang, and Namhae. Therefore, I sent official dispatches to both Cholla Right Naval Station Commander Yi Ok-ki and Kyongsang Right Naval Station Commander Won Kyun to take united action with me. As a result, we captured the enemy vessels and cut off the heads of his officers and men and destroyed them altogether before we returned to our respective headquarters on the 10th of sixth moon as I have already reported.

When I received from the Joint Border-Defense Council an official letter transmitting Your Majesty's written orders I pledged anew with the two Commanders and sent official dispatches to annihilate the individual raiders who frequent our shores and islands, as I assembled my warships in battle formation.

As a result of reconnaissance of the enemy movements in Kyongsang Province, it has come to my knowledge that the Japanese vessels in groups of ten to thirty frequent the islands of Kadok and Koje, and I have also heard that the Japanese ground troops invaded Kumsan in Cholla Province. In this way, the enemy is extending his attacks on land and sea, but no one rises to resist. Should things go on this way, the enemy will march farther and deeper north through the heartland of our country. Therefore, in the evening of the 4th of seventh moon I led my fleet to the appointed rendezvous agreed upon with Yi Ok-ki, Commander of Cholla Right Naval Station. On the fifth we renewed our pledge to fight, and on the sixth I led our united fleet to Noryang on the boundary of Konyang and Namhae, and saw Won Kyun, Commander of Kyongsang Right Naval Station, who had been staying there with seven damaged warships barely repaired. We met at sea for a strategic conference, and sailed to Changsin-do, where we passed the night. On the seventh a strong easterly wind arose and navigation was difficult. On reaching Tangpo at nightfall our men gathered wood and drew water, when Kim Chon-son, a cowherd on that island came running toward our warships and reported, "Over seventy enemy vessels large, medium, and small, sailed from the sea off Yongdungpo today at 2:00 p.m., and entered Kyonnaeryang, where they are now riding at anchor." I ordered my ships' captains to be on the alert, and early on the morning of the eighth we set out to sea. As we looked toward the enemy anchorage, two enemy vanguard vessels, large and medium, came out, spied our ships and returned to their positions. We immediately chased them and found eighty-two enemy vessels (36 large, 34 medium, 12 small) lined up in a long row, but the channel of Kyonnaeryang was narrow and strewn with sunken rocks so it was not only difficult to fight in the bay for fear our board-roofed ships might collide with one another but also the enemy might escape to land by jumping ashore when driven into a corner. For these reasons, I adopted the tactic of luring the enemy out to the sea in front of Hansando where we could capture his vessels and slaughter his men in strike, because Hansando lies between Koje and Kosong, separated all round from land to swim to, and even those who landed would die of starvation.

First, I ordered out five or six board-roofed vanguard ships to make chase, feigning a surprise attack. When the enemy vessels under full sail pursued our ships, they fled from the bay as if returning to base. The enemy vessels kept pursuing ours until they came out to open sea. Immediately I commanded my ships' captain to line up in the Crane Wing formation so as to surround the enemy vessels in a semi-circle. Then I roared "Charge!" Our ships dashed forward with the roar of cannons "Earth," "Black," and "Victory," breaking two or three of the enemy vessels into pieces. The other enemy vessels, stricken with terror, scattered and fled in all directions in great confusion. Our officers and men and local officials on board shouted "Victory!" and darted at flying speed, vying with one another, as they hailed down arrows and bullets like a thunder storm, burning the enemy vessels and slaughtering his warriors completely...

...In addition, the remaining enemy vessels (20 large, 17 medium, and 5 small) were broken and burnt by the united attacks of scores of our warriors from the Right and Left Naval Stations. Countless numbers of Japanese were hit by arrows and fell dead into the water.

However, about four hundred exhausted Japanese, finding no way to escape, deserted their boats and fled ashore, while the remaining Japanese boats (one large, seven medium, and six small) which had fallen behind during the battle, seeing from afar the horrible sight of burning vessels and falling heads, rowed their boats very fast and fled in all directions. Both officers and men on our ships were exhausted by the fierce day-long battle, and the gathering dusk made it impossible for us to pursue the escaping Japanese to the end, so we returned to our position in the inner sea of Kyonnaeryang to rest for the night...

...I fear that the enemy might return in a second invasion with reinforcements and attack us from both flanks. Therefore, before breaking up our combined fleet, I agreed with Yi Ok-ki, Commander of Cholla Right Naval Station, to keep our sailors on the alert, with bows and spears beside them, waking for sleeping, to be ready when an emergency rises once again.

I also gave instructions to the local officials to give relief to the persons who have been recaptured and to send them home when peace is restored.

The recent victories were won thanks to the united strength of commanders, sailors, and local officials. At the present time, the Royal

Headquarters is far away, and traffic is blocked. If the war exploits of our valiant officers and men are graded and announced after the arrival of the government orders, the delay would not be good for morale. Therefore, in consideration of what they achieved in battle I have marked the order of their individual merit by three classes – A, B, & C... on the list of their names in the appendix. The officers and men are placed on the record with marks they deserve in line with my promise, even though they did not cut off many enemy heads.

Yi, Commander
15th of Seventh Moon, 1592

Memorials to Court: 20. Request for Order to Settle War Refugees on Tolsando Farms

I memorialize the throne on the following matter for reference.

There are about two hundred families of wandering war refugees who fled from Kyongsang Province and live in the districts under the jurisdiction of my Navy Headquarters. These refugees were given accommodations in temporary quarters to pass the winter, but there is no way to get supplies for their relief, and even though they can return to their native homes when peace is restored no one can bear to see them die of starvation in the meantime. Following my letter addressed to Chief State Councilor Yu Song-nyong, an official dispatch arrived from the Border Defense Command, "If there are arable lands on the islands suitable for agriculture, send the refugees to those islands to cultivate crops and make a living thereon. Take proper measures for the establishment of farm villages as you deem fit." After careful survey I have found that no other islands are preferable to Tolsando, because this island lies between my naval station (in Yosu) and

Pangtap, which is protected by high mountains all around its vast fertile plains, and inaccessible to thieves or sea-rovers. I have instructed the refugees to enter the island and to commence the spring plowing, which they did with gladness.

When former Royal Supreme Commissioner Hong Chong-nok, Governor Yun Tu-su, Naval Commanders Pak Son, Yi Ch'on, and Yi Yong memorialized the throne about farm cultivation by border guards at my Navy Headquarters, the Ministry of War objected to the plan for the reason that agriculture would interfere with horse-breeding on that island. Now that the country is at war and many people have lost their livelihood, and in any case, the tilling of soil by wandering refugees will not do any harm to horse-breeding, it is earnestly hoped that a royal decree be issued to facilitate both horse-breeding and refugee relief.

Yi, Commander
26th of First Moon, 1593

War Dairy: September 3, 1594

Drizzled. At dawn I received a confidential letter from the King's court. It says "The generals on land and the admirals at sea have folded their arms as they look at each other's faces without making any single plan to proceed or to attack the enemy." I should like to reply, "No such thing in my sea-life during the past three years. Though I swore with other captains of war to avenge our slaughtered countrymen upon the enemy by risking our own lives, and we pass many days on land and at sea in this resolution, the enemy has taken his positions in deep trenches and high fortresses on steep hills inaccessible to us. It is not wise to proceed frivolously. A wise captain of war should keep to the rule "Knowing yourself and knowing the enemy is the surest way to secure success in a hundred battles." A strong wind blew all day. From early in the evening I sat in candle light all alone. As I think of the state affairs in utter confusion and disturbance, there seems nobody in the central government who could save the nation from danger. What should be done? Seeing that I sat up alone until ten o'clock, Hungyang came in and talked with me deep into midnight before he retired from my presence.

War Diary: July 1, 1595

Showers. Being a national memorial service day (for King Injong) I did not attend office; sitting alone in my pavilion, I thought of the nation power as if as ephemeral as the morning dew; there does not seem to be any eminent minister who can make positive decisions within, nor is there a general who can save the nation without. I cannot even guess what will become of the nation. My thoughts are perplexed; I tossed and rolled in deep thought.

War Diary: September 15, 1597 [A day before the Battle of Myongnyang]

Clear. By riding the rising tide I led the Captains of all ships to move to the sea off Usuyong, because it was not right for a small fleet to take a fighting position with its back against Myongnyang (Ultolmok, the Roaring Channel), whose swift current falls like a cataract behind Pyokpajong (the Sea-Viewing Pavilion). Calling my Staff Officers and all ships' Captains, I gave the following instruction: "According to the principles of strategy, 'He who seeks his death shall live, he who seeks his life shall die.' Again, the strategy says 'If one defender stands on watch at a strong gateway he may drive terror deep into the heart of the enemy coming by the ten thousand.' These are golden sayings for us. You Captains are expected to strictly obey my orders. If you do not, even the least error shall not be pardoned, but shall be severely punished by Martial Law." In this way I showed them my firm attitude. In my dream this night a spirit appeared before me and declared, "If you do in this way, you shall win a great victory; if you do in that way you shall suffer a tragic defeat."

War Diary: September 16, 1597 [The day of the Battle of Myongnyang]

Clear. Early in the morning, a special scouting unit reported "The enemy vessels in countless numbers, having passed the Channel of Myongnyang, enter the area where we have our positions." At once I ordered all ships in my fleet, including my Flagship, to weigh anchor and I led them out to sea. Soon after, one hundred and thirty odd enemy vessels enveloped us. Our ships' Captains lost their fighting morale at the sight of the enemy's overwhelming strength of numbers, and used various devices to fall out from the line of battle. In particular, the ship of Kim Ok-chu, Commander of the Cholla Right Naval Station, had already fallen away to a distance of over one mile. I had our oarsmen row the Flagship swiftly and dash forward like an arrow while our gunners at my signal poured down fire on the enemy vessels from our "Earth" and "Black" type Cannons. The cannon balls burst on the enemy vessels like a hailstorm, and the fire arrows flying from the bows of men standing on the Flagship fell like rain. Before this attack the enemy only milled around and did not dash against us. Being surrounded two and three deep by the enemy vessels, however, the officers and men on our ship looked at each other with fear. At this time I reassured them once again in a quiet voice "The enemy vessels are many, but they cannot come to attack us. Have no fear, but shoot at them with all your might." Then I looked around for our ships, which had fallen far astern. I thought of turning the bow of my Flagship to issue my commands, but if I did, the enemy vessels will come nearer and I would find myself between the devil and the deep sea – impossible to advance or turn back. Just then a fresh idea flashed in my mind. I blew a horn and ordered my Staff Officers to raise a military command flag together with a call signal, accompanied by shell trumpets, then the ship of Kim Ung-ham, Commandant of Mijohang and the leader of the central squadron drew nearer to my Flagship, preceded by the ship of An Wi, the Magistrate of Koje. Standing on the bridge of my Flagship, I roared, "An Wi! Do you wish to die at my order? An Wi, do you wish to die under court martial? If you escape, where can you find a place to live?" Then An Wi, inspired, plunged into the line of battle. Next, I called Kim Ung-ham, and roared "As leader of the central squadron, you fell far astern and would not come to the rescue of your Commanding Admiral. How can you escape from your guilt?" I wanted to execute him right away, but since the attacking enemy was so near and so dangerous, I gave him an opportunity to redeem himself with a fine military feat. As the two ships were darting toward the enemy position, the enemy's flagship ordered two boats under its command to attack, then the enemy hordes like black ants climbed up An Wi's ship. Seeing this, An Wi's sailors fought them off desperately with sharp-edged clubs, long spears, or sea-washed stones until all the fighters were exhausted. I ordered my men to turn the bow of my Flagship and to dash forward under cover of gunfire and fire-arrows. In a moment three enemy vessels were burnt and turned over. Then the ships of Nokto (Song Yo-jong, captain) and Pyongsanpo Acting Captain Cong Ung-tu, came to reinforce our ships and killed off the enemy warriors remaining on board. On my Flagship there was a surrendered Japanese named

Toshisuna, who came from the enemy's camp in Angol. When he looked down at the enemy soldiers and sailors swimming in blood on the surface of the sea, he caught sight of a man wearing a red brocade uniform embroidered with flower crests, and cried "It is, it is Matashi, the Japanese general in Angol!" I ordered Kim Tolson, a water carrier on my ship, to hook up the floating body onto the hatchway. Then Toshisuna leaped with joy and shouted "I am positive, it is he – Matashi!" I commanded my men to cut the body into pieces and, from that time the morale of the enemy was greatly affected. Knowing that the enemy could come to fight us no more, our ships, beating drums and shouting battle cries, darted forward, and attacked the enemy vessels, shooting of cannons marked "Earth" and "Black," whose bursting detonations shook the seas and the mountains. Together with the rain of arrows, they destroyed thirty-one enemy vessels in this single battle. The enemy scattered and fled to return no more. We wished to pass the night on the field of battle, but the waves were extremely rough and an adverse wind was blowing hard, making the area dangerous. Therefore we moved out formation to Tangsado to stop overnight. The victory was really made with heavenly aid.

The Warships and Weaponry of Korea and Japan

During the Imjin War, the Korean Navy used both Panokson and Kobukson warships. The Panokson was the mainstay of the navy, while one to three Kobukson would be used as the main assault ships. The ships of the Japanese Navy consisted of the large *Atake*, the medium-sized *Sekibune* and the smaller *Kobaya*. The Atake served as the flagship, carrying on board the commanding admirals, while the medium-sized Sekibune comprised the greater part of the rest of the navy.

A key feature of the Panokson was its multiple decks. The non-combatant personnel were positioned between the main-deck and the upper-deck, away from enemy fire. The combatant personnel were stationed on the upper-deck, which allowed them to attack the enemy from a higher vantage point. The Japanese fleet serviced mostly single-decked vessels, with the exception of a few large Atakes.

In line with the traditional structure of Korean ships, the Panokson had a flat base. This feature was due to the nature of the Korean seacoast, which had a broad tidal range and flat, expansive tidelands. A level underside enabled a ship to sit comfortably on the tideland when the tide was out, after coming ashore or inside a wharf at high water. It also ensured greater mobility and a light draft and in particular allowed a ship to make sharp changes of direction at short notice. This Panokson was one of the main reasons why Admiral Yi was able to employ the Crane Wing formation at the Battle of Hansando with such success.

By contrast, the hulls of the Japanese vessels were V-shaped. A sharp underside was favorable for swift or long-distance travel because of lower water resistance. Since this variety of hull had a deep draft, however, the ship's turning radius was considerable and changing direction was therefore a lengthy process.

Both Korean and Japanese ships used sails and oars. Of the two basic types of sail, square and lateen, the square gives a strong performance downwind but struggles windward, whereas the fore-and-aft lateen sail excels against the wind, though requiring a large crew to handle it. In the West, square sails were used in the galleys of Ancient Greece and the Viking longships, and the fore-and-aft variety later in the Mediterranean ships of the Late Middle Ages. When the Age of Exploration began in the fifteenth century, multiple-masted ships equipped with both types of sails eventually appeared. In Korea such ships had been in use since the eighth century. Korea's Panokson and Kobukson therefore had two masts by default, and their position and angle could easily be managed so that the sails could be used in all winds, whether adverse or favorable.[4] The Atake of the Japanese Navy also had two masts, but the main parts of its vessels were square-rigged and their sails limited to use in favorable winds.

It is worthwhile also to compare the hulls of the two nations' respective warships, and their relative strength. The Panokson used thick high density boards, giving an overall sturdiness to the ship's structure. Japanese warships were weaker, due to the thin, lower density timber used to build them.[5] The Sekibune in particular, being the standard warship of the

---

[4] Korea employed multiple-masted ships from the Silla period (BC 57 – AD 935). A Japanese record states that the ships used by Paekche and merchant ships of Chang Pogo of Silla had multiple masts. The superior performance of such ships came to be known to China also, and an ancient Chinese text *Defending the Seas: A Discussion* explains that "The turtle-shaped ship of Korea can raise and lay down its sail at will, and it can travel with equal ease whether the wind is adverse or the tide low."

[5] The main type of timber traditionally used in Korea for shipbuilding is pine; to increase its strength oak, in particular the evergreen, was often used. Korean pine

Korean Panokson

Japanese fleet, was built to be as light as possible, increasing its speed at the expense of structural integrity.

The Panokson was not only built using thicker timbers, but its general structure was held together by means of wooden nails, matching indentations and interlocking teeth. This meant that as its boards absorbed water and expanded, the greater integrity of the hull was made stronger. The Japanese warships, on the other hand, relied on metal nails which, as time passed and corrosion and rust set in, eventually weakened the hull.

This difference in structural integrity, which also determined the

---

often has knots and bends, and because it was dangerous to process such a tree into thin timber, it was processed thickly to reinforce the strength. Traditional Japanese ships were commonly made out of the Japanese cedar or fir, which are lighter and easier to process than pine. Capitalizing on this, traditional Japanese ships have been built out of timber processed thinly and accurately. But strength-wise, cedars and firs suffer from the drawback of being weaker than pine. This in the end meant that Japanese ships were built out of weak material processed thinly, while Korean ships with strong material processed into thick timber.

Japanese Atake

number of cannons that could be carried on board, suited Japan and Korea to different types of naval combat. Because the Japanese ships lacked the strength to withstand the recoil of cannon, even the largest ship Atake could carry only three at the most. Since the hulls of Korean warships were strong enough, however, they were able to carry a large number of long-range cannons. These could be installed with ease on the large upper-deck of the Panokson ships, and their angle configured at will to increase the range.

Since the Japanese warships only allowed for a very limited number of cannons, their sailors mainly used muskets, which had a range of 100-200m (330-660 ft). Korea, on the other hand, had on board several varieties of cannon, such as Heaven, Earth, Black and Yellow. They fired *taejon* (a long, thick arrow in the shape of a rocket) with a range of 500m (1,650 ft), as well as *chulwhan* (cannon shot) which could travel up to a distance of 1km (3300 ft). Wangu, a kind of mortar, which fired stones or shells with a radius of 20cm (7.8 in), was also used by the Korean Navy.

Another noteworthy aspect of Korea's heavy fire-arms is that they were not all invented to meet the sudden emergency of war. These weapons in fact made their appearance some 200 years prior to the Imjin War. Korean cannons first saw action at sea in 1380 against a large fleet of Japanese pirate ships, and were found to be a great success. In comparison, the first naval battle to have employed cannons in Europe was the Battle of Lepanto (1571), 200 years later.

In the 15th century, under the lead of King Sejong, who was himself a pioneer of scientific research, the performance of these heavy artilleries improved dramatically. Having built a cannon range next to the Royal Court, and after much experimentation and study, King Sejong finally increased the extent of the cannons' firepower from 300m (980 ft) to 1800m (60,000 ft). Naval canons were also developed at this time and among them, Heaven, Earth, Black, and Yellow cannon were later employed by Yi Sun-sin. The development of artillery steadily continued after King Sejong, and saw the invention of the *Pikok Chinchonloe*, a time-bomb that flung out hundreds of metal shards upon explosion, and the *Tapoki*, a machine capable of firing many arrows at once.

The main naval strategy employed by the Japanese was that of "grapple-and-board," whereby sailors would attempt to board an enemy ship and fall to sword fighting on the decks. The Japanese Navy's concept of sea battle was therefore one of a fight between crews rather than the vessels themselves. This was the most common naval strategy in the world during this time, and was as common among the Europeans of the day. The Korean Navy, however, utilizing superior warships and firepower to burn and sink the enemy vessels, engaged in a more modern type of naval warfare.

Comparison between Korean and Japanese Warships

	Korean Warship	Japanese Warship
Hull	U-shaped with level base Quick to change direction thanks to small turning radius	V-shaped Greater potential for speed but large turning radius
Crew	Panokson: 120-200 Kobukson: 150	Atake: 200-300 Sekibune: 100 Kobaya: 40
Speed	3 knots	3 knots minimum
Sail	Multiple-masts: sails could be used both windward and downwind	Square-sail: limited to downwind use
Timber	Pine and Oak	Japanese Cedar and Fir
Joints	Wooden nail: expands in water to strengthen overall structure	Metal nail: corrodes in water weakening overall structure
Main Weapon	Heavy artillery: range 500m (1,650 ft) Fire-arrows	Muskets: range 200m (660ft) Spears, swords, arrows
Method of Attack	Breaching enemy hulls Burning and sinking enemy ships	Grappling and Boarding Killing and wounding enemy crews

Interior of the Kobukson I

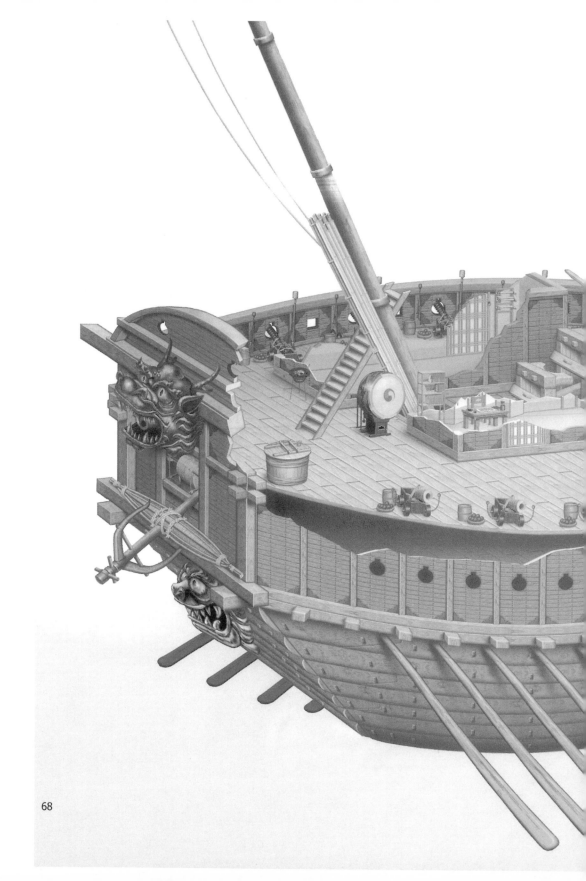

Interior of the Kobukson II

The Admiralship of Yi Sun-sin

Following are some of the key features of Admiral Yi Sun-sin's leadership that lead to his legendary naval victories.

1. Thorough preparation and intensive training

Before the war and throughout it, and even during the truce, Admiral Yi always subjected his men to intensive training in archery, artillery, and the various standard naval maneuvers and formations. He also tirelessly engaged himself in manufacturing new weapons and building ships. For example, only a year after the Battle of Myongnyang which he fought with a mere thirteen ships, he had succeeded in building 70 more – an astonishing rate of one new ship per every five days.

2. Careful study of the nature of the battlefield and its layout

The southern coast of Korea, the scene of many fierce sea battles between Korea and Japan during the Imjin War, was a maritime labyrinth, consisting of countless isles and inlets. Furthermore, the current in that region is very fast and the long stretching coast provided a completely different appearance with the rise and fall of every tide. Yi made a careful study of the hourly changes of currents and winds, as well as the natural features peculiar to each naval battlefield. Based on his investigations, he was able to rely on a safe sea-route whenever he moved his fleet at night, escaping the eye of the enemy. As evident from the battles fought at Hansando and Myongnyang, his foreknowledge allowed him to turn the complex geographical features of the coast to his advantage when pursuing or being pursued by an enemy.

3. Diverse use of naval tactics

Admiral Yi used a wide variety of naval tactics in sea battles besides the famous Crane Wing formation[6]. In his first battle at Okpo, he arranged his fleet in horizontal line and made straight for the enemy fleet at full speed, thus not allowing them the least room to maneuver or escape and pressing them close with fierce cannon fire. In the sea battle at Pusan, the Long Snake formation (Kor. Changsa-jin) was used in order to deal with the formidable odds – 83 Korean ships against 480 Japanese. Yi adopted this long, narrow formation to minimize the exposure of his fleet to the enemy's fire. Korea emerged victorious from this battle, sinking 128 enemy ships and losing none herself. In the Battle of Happo, Yi's fleet droved the enemy fleet into a confined harbor, and was thus able to destroy all of its ships. In that engagement, Yi had no need to use formal naval formations, but simply ordered his ships to dash forward individually against the enemy as he judged fit.

---

[6] According to *Right Naval Station Warfare Formations with Illustrations* published in 1780, over ten naval formations were used by the Korean Navy such as the Command, the Crane Wing, the Little Crane, the Straight, the Diamond, the Wedge, the Right Left Chal, the Circle, the Curvature and the Two Line.

4. Undermining enemy morale and winning the trust of his men

During naval engagements, Yi's navy subjected the enemy to a bombardment of arrows and cannon shot from the outset, a tactic which proved highly effective in weakening the enemy's fighting morale, and finally getting the better of them. As a consequence, Korean sailors developed an absolute trust in their admiral, and their morale grew higher and higher with every victory to which he led them.

5. Maintaining perfect discipline and strict principles

Lazy officers were rewarded with strokes of the cudgel, regardless of their rank. Soldiers who deserted the army were punished with death, as were officers who accepted bribes and overlooked their desertion, and indeed any man who was found to have committed the same crime more than once. At the Battle of Myongnyang, Yi angrily reproved An Wi, who had fallen back out of fear, threatening him with death under court martial if he did not heed his call to advance, and his words awakened An Wi to recover his spirit and fight. Admiral Yi's emphasis on strict obedience to martial law and the maintenance of absolute discipline meant that the whole Korean Navy, from the supreme commander to the common soldier, were firmly united as one and were thus able to carry out the naval formations and tactics which demanded strong unity among crew members successfully.

6. Fellowship and Duty

Although Chinese Admiral Chen Lien had attempted to hinder Yi's plan to destroy the retreating Japanese force, the admiral rescued Chen when he was encircled by enemy ships at Noryang and in danger of being captured. In the Battle of Myongnyang, An Wi abandoned his loyalty to his commander at the sight of the enemy's overwhelming numbers, but was later saved by the admiral when he fell into trouble. Yi was always faithful to his principles and would not permit injustice or irresponsibility in his men. But at the same time, he harbored a deep sense of fellowship and obligation to them and so gained their trust, respect, and devoted service.

7. Leadership overcame the worst conditions

Throughout the Imjin War, Admiral Yi alone undertook to provide for every aspect of warfare, from supplies and provisions to recruitment and shipbuilding, having no support from the government. In battles where overwhelming odds were involved, he led his navy from the front to inspire his men with his valor and zeal. In the desperate situation before the Battle of Myongnyang, when the Korean Navy had only thirteen ships with which to fight, Yi was able to re-arm his men, with the dauntless soldier's maxim "He who seeks death will live, and he who seeks life will die."

Behind all these methods and devices lie Yi's unshakable loyalty and selfless dedication to his country and people. In the course of abiding by them, Yi had to endure endless trials and sufferings. He remained loyal to his country, however, even after imprisonment, torture, and ignominious demotion to the ranks, since he firmly believed that remaining at sea and defeating the enemy was the one thing he could do for his nation. It is this splendid patriotic devotion that could be seen as the most powerful and important strategy of Admiral Yi Sun-sin.

Yi Sun-sin: His Memories and Influence on Korea Today

Even after 400 years, the noble spirit of Admiral Yi, which saved a country from the brink of collapse, remains as the object of veneration and admiration. The following are a selection of different ways in which the admiral has been remembered by his countrymen since his valiant death at the Battle of Noryang.

1. King Sonjo, expressing his apologies and praying for the soul of Yi, gave the following funeral address.

> I abandoned you, and yet
> You did not once abandon me.
> The sufferings you underwent in this world,
> And those you take with you to the world after,
> How could one convey them in words?

Later, in 1604, the 37th year of Sonjo's reign, Yi was honored posthumously as the Vice-Prime Minister. In 1643, the 27th year of King Injo's reign, he was awarded the posthumous title 'Chung Mu Gong' (Master of Loyal Valor). In 1793, the 17th year of King Chongjo's reign, he was honored posthumously as the Prime Minister.

Under the Royal Ordinance of King Chongjo, an exhaustive compilation of the deeds and achievements of Yi's lifetime was undertaken in 1793. Entitled *A Complete Collection on Chung Mu Gong Yi*, it was published in 14 volumes after three years of research. Assigned and protected as the cultural heritage, the collection is an important historical source which illuminates all of Yi's legacies to Korea.

2. Numerous shrines and monuments dedicated to the admiral's memory have been built, including the Asan Memorial Shrine. All over the southern part of Korea, where vestiges of his footmarks remain – at the sites of his various battles, at Cholla Naval Station, at his training camps and so on – the public continue to visit and pay their respects.

The world's first ironclad warship, the Kobukson, was restored and reconstructed by the Korean Navy in 1980, and placed on exhibit in the Republic of Korea Naval Academy, Asan Memorial Shrine, The War Memorial, and Chinju National Museum.

The scientific innovation behind Yi's Kobukson is the spiritual foundation and driving force behind the shipbuilding industry in Korea today. Over 30% of the world's ships are built in Korean shipyards, and its marine technology is regarded as the most sophisticated in the world. In terms of order volume, it continues to stay ahead of its nearest competitor Japan as it has done for many years.

3. Admiral Yi is one of the most respected figures in Korean history and there are no fewer than 200 books written on him, with 74 published in 2004 and 2005 alone. The biographical novel *Song of the Sword*, based on the story of the admiral's life, became a bestseller and was even singled out as recommended reading by Korea's former President Roh Mu-hyun.

4. Since the beginning of the 21st century, many Koreans have become keen to learn the attitude and methods of Yi Sun-sin for their own development. His integrity, loyalty and devotion, his fine strategies, creative thinking, painstaking forward-planning and emphasis on the gathering of information through contacts all fulfill the criteria demanded of a leader in modern times. The field of economics and management is just one area in which the study and application of Yi's strategies and leadership has taken root. Professor Ji

Yong-hee, author of *In Times of Economical Warfare: A Meeting with Yi Sun-sin*, is currently giving lectures under the series title 'Yi Sun-sin on Business Management.' Regarding Yi as a model for 21st century leadership, he argues there are many lessons we can learn from him, including being faithful to basics, establishing trust between individuals, striving for innovation, valuing information, and not falling victim to pride. Professor Ji says, "Yi, above all, was strict with his own self, and he stood by his principles till the very end, thereby earning the trust of those around him. Today this might be called 'Transparent Management.' Since he founded himself on morality, his subordinates believed and trusted him absolutely. He was moreover very modest. And since modest, he was always prepared."

5. Even in the sphere of culture, Yi has emerged as an iconic figure of 21st century Korea. The television show "The Immortal Yi Sun-sin" had its debut on September 4, 2004, went on to receive the record ratings of almost 30%, and was voted as one of the most popular broadcasts of the year. Its success in the East generated considerable interest in the United States, and a subtitled version was soon released for American audiences.

6. Admiral Yi is before all else a symbol of pride and inspiration to the Korean Navy. To this day, much research takes place on his tactics and leadership methods at the Republic of Korea Naval Academy, Republic of Korea Navy, the Naval Education & Training Command, and the Republic of Korea Marine Corps.

Naval Battles of Admiral Yi Sun-sin

During the Imjin War, Yi Sun-sin had engaged in twenty-three naval battles against Japan and emerged victorious in all of them. The naval battles fought by the Admiral are summarized in the following chart.

	Date Month/Day/Year	Location	Korean Ships	Japanese Ships	Outcome
1	5/7/1592	Okpo	27	26	26 enemy ships sunk
2	5/7/1592	Happo	27	5	5 enemy ships sunk
3	5/8/1592	Chokjinpo	27	13	11 enemy ships sunk
4	5/29/1592	Sachon	26	13	13 enemy ships sunk
5	6/2/1592	Tangpo	27	21	21 enemy ships sunk
6	6/5/1592	Tanghangpo	51	26	26 enemy ships sunk
7	6/7/1592	Yulpo	51	7	7 enemy ships sunk
8	7/8/1592	Hansando-do	56	73	47 enemy ships sunk 12 enemy ships captured
9	7/10/1592	Angolpo	56	42	42 enemy ships sunk
10	8/29/1592	Changrimpo	81	6	6 enemy ships sunk
11	9/1/1592	Hwajungumi	81	5	5 enemy ships sunk
12	9/1/1592	Tadaepo	81	8	8 enemy ships sunk
13	9/1/1592	Sopyongpo	81	9	9 enemy ships sunk

14	9/1/1592	Cholyong-do	81	2	2 enemy ships sunk
15	9/1/1592	Choryangmok	81	4	4 enemy ships sunk
16	9/1/1592	Pusanpo	81	470	128 enemy ships sunk
17	3/4/1594	Chinhae	30	10	10 enemy ships sunk
18	3/5/1594	Tanghangpo	124	50	21 enemy ships sunk
19	9/29/1594	Changmunpo	50	117	2 enemy ships sunk
20	9/16/1597	Myongnyang	13	330	31 enemy ships sunk 90 enemy ships severely damaged
21	7/18/1598	Choli-do	?	100	50 enemy ships sunk
22	9/20/1598	Chang-do	211 (Korea 83+ China 128)	?	30 enemy ships sunk 11 enemy ships captured
23	11/18/1598	Noryang	146 (Korea 83 + China 63)	500	450 enemy ships sunk

In addition to the twenty-three sea battles, several minor engagements took place. These include an assault by the Korean Navy on the Japanese naval base, and its successful defense of its own camp from the Japanese.

	Date Month/Day/Year	Location	Korean Ships	Japanese Ships	Outcome
1	2/10/1593 ~3/6/1593	Wungchon	89	40	100 enemy sailors killed
2	10/4/1594	Changmumpo	50	?	Japanese Retreat

3	8/28/1597	Eoranjin	12	8	Japanese Retreat
4	9/7/1597	Pyokpajin	12	13	Japanese Retreat
5	11/13/1598	Chang-do	146 (Korea 83 + China 63)	10	Japanese Retreat

Won Kyun had been instated as the Supreme Naval Commander in Yi's place while he was serving as a common foot soldier, and led three sea battles which ended in the Korean Navy's worst catastrophe.

	Date Month/Day/Year	Location	Korean Ships	Japanese Ships	Outcome
1	7/7/1597	Cholyong-do	168	500	7 Korean ships sunk & captured
2	7/9/1597	Kadok	161	1000	27 Korean Ships sunk & captured
3	7/16/1597	Chilchonnyang	134	1000	122 Korean ships sunk & captured

* All dates are based on lunar calendar, which was used in East Asia until the late nineteenth century.

* The number of ships involved and the outcome of each naval engagement as shown in the charts have been taken from Admiral Yi's *War Diary* and *Memorials to Court*, as well as from the *Royal Annals of the Choson Dynasty (Kor. Choson Wangjo Sillok)*, the official record compiled by the government.

* Throughout the Imjin War, the Korean Navy under Admiral Yi suffered

some casualties but lost no ships in action; only two ships were lost by the mistake of captains on their way back to the naval base after the battle at Wungchon. Such overwhelming victories by the Korean Navy may be attributed to the structural integrity of their ships, built in durable design and material, and the superior firepower and range of their naval artillery. The Japanese warships, limited by weaker design, could only carry at most three cannons with much less firepower, and their main weaponry muskets were effective in killing enemy sailors but not in destroying enemy ships. Yi thus utilized the strategy of sinking the enemy warship with concentrated cannon-fire before the distance between their ships had narrowed down to the musket range of 200m. In short, the Korean Navy could achieve successes unparalleled in the history of naval warfare due to Yi's forceful strategy that fully realized the superiority of Korean ships and guns.

* Of the twenty three battles Yi had fought, the largest and the fiercest was the Battle of Noryang, the final engagement that put the 146 ships of Korea and China against the 500 of Japan carrying back their entire army on retreat home. The long, seven-year war, originating from the delusive ambition of a man in search for fame and territory, had taken away countless innocent lives and utterly destroyed their homeland. Boarding every supply and weapon he had onto warships, Yi headed for Noryang to carry out his final duty for his country and people. He took off his armor and helmet and fought at the heart of the battle, firing arrows and beating the war drums himself. He had never before taken off his armor or helmet in action. Perhaps it had been his resolve to end his difficult, arduous life with this last victory at sea. When he died by an enemy bullet, neither his crews nor the Chinese Navy knew of his death. They poured their hearts and souls into defeating the enemy till the very end and achieved the resounding victory that saw the sinking of 450 Japanese warships out of 500. It was the most

honorable and precious victory for the Korean Navy earned in sacrifice of the admiral's life.

With his last breath, he said, "Tell no one of my death." He was concerned that his death might encumber the fighting against the enemy.

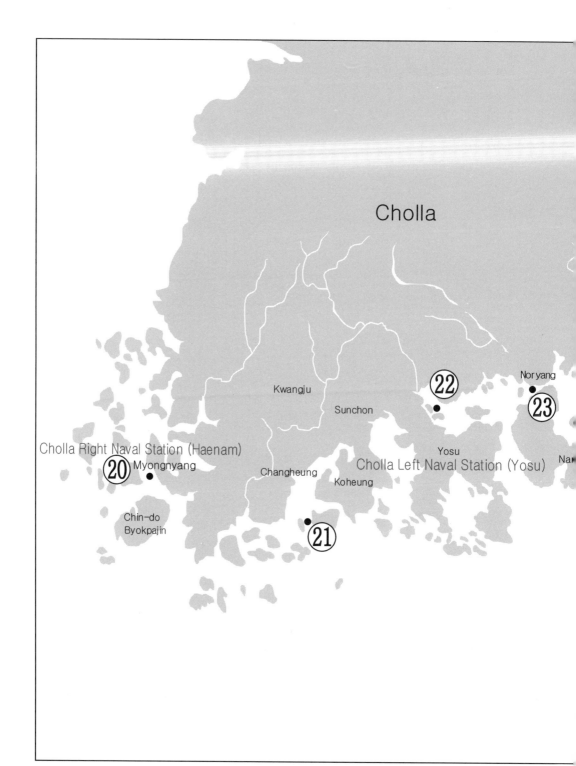

Cholla

Noryang

㉒

㉓

Kwangju

Sunchon

Cholla Right Naval Station (Haenam)

Yosu

Cholla Left Naval Station (Yosu)   Na

㉒

Myongnyang

Changheung

Koheung

Chin-do
Byokpajin

㉑

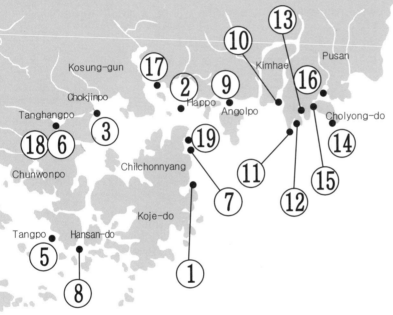

Kyongsang

Kosung-gun

Chokjinpo

Tanghangpo

Chunwonpo

Chilchonnyang

Koje-do

Tangpo   Hansan-do

Happo

Angolpo

Kimhae

Pusan

Cholyong-do

Naval Battles of Admiral Yi

① Okpo
② Happo
③ Chokjinpo
④ Sachon
⑤ Tangpo
⑥ Tanghangpo

⑦ Yulpo
⑧ Hansan-do
⑨ Angolpo
⑩ Changrimpo
⑪ Hwajungumi
⑫ Tadaepo

⑬ Sopyongpo
⑭ Cholyong-do
⑮ Choryangmok
⑯ Pusanpo
⑰ Chinhae
⑱ Tanghangpo II

⑲ Changmunpo
⑳ Myongnyang
㉑ Choli-do
㉒ Chang-do
㉓ Noryang

Chronological Career Note

1545. 8th day of 3rd moon. One o'clock in the morning Yi Sun-sin was born as the third son of Chong at his home at Konchon-dong, Seoul. His clan origin was Toksu; his mother was of the Pyon clan. His mother had a dream before she brought forth her third son: Her father-in-law appeared in her dream and advised as follows: "You will have a son who will be a great man and his name shall be 'Sun-sin'."

1552. His family moved to Asan, the country home of the family.

1564. Married to the daughter of Pang Chin, a military officer.

1566. Started practice in archery and drilling necessary for military service.

1567. His first son, Hoe was born.

1571. His second son, Yol was born.

1572. In the 8th moon. He fell from horseback and broke his left leg while he was taking the military service examination.

1576. 2nd moon. Passed military service examination. 12th moon. Appointed the Acting Commandant of Fortress Tonggubi, Hamgyung Province.

1577. Third son, Myon was born.

1579. Appointed staff captain to the Army Commander of Chungchong Province.

1580. 7th moon. Appointed Naval commandant of Palpo, Cholla Province.

1583. 7th moon. Staff officer of the Hamgyong Army Commander.

10th moon. Appointed Acting Commander of Konwon Fortress, and destroyed the Jurchen forces.

11th moon. Appointed Staff Officer of Military Training Command.

15th day of 11th moon. His father Chong passed away.

Resigned his official post in accordance with the custom of the society, which required a mourner to withdraw himself from official posts for two years.

1586. Appointed Garrison Captain of Chosan Fortress, Hamgyung Province.

1587. Dismissed from the post and enlisted as common soldier owing to the jealousy of Yi Il, Army Commander of Hamgyung.

1588. 6th moon. Returned home.

1589. 2nd moon. Appointed Staff Officer of Cholla Commissioner.

11th moon. Appointed Concurrent Transmitter-Commissioner.

12th moon. Appointed Magistrate of Chongup Prefecture.

1591. 13th day of 2nd moon. Appointed Navy Commander of Left Cholla Province.

1592. Completed the Turtle Ship before the Hideyoshi Invasion started.

13th day of 4th moon. Japanese forces invaded Korea.

5th moon. The first campaign at Okpo with the signal victory of the Admiral.

6th moon. The second campaign at Tangpo with the victory of the Admiral.

7th moon. Defeated the Japanese Navy in the Hansando campaign.

9th moon. Fourth campaign at Busan-po with his victory.

1593. 2nd moon. Defeated Japanese fleet at Ungpo.

7th moon. Moved his fleet to Hansando-do.

8th moon. Appointed Tongjesa, Supreme Naval Commander of the Three Provinces.

1594. 7th day of 3rd moon. Submitted his objection to the peace negotiation proposed by Ming Chinese envoy Tan.

6th of 4th moon. Held provisional Military Examination at Hansando-do to recruit sailors.

9th moon. Defeated the enemy at Changmunpo.

1595. 2nd moon. Submitted a memorial to be transferred from his present post because of the criticism by Admiral Won Kyun. Refused.

1597. 2nd moon. Placed under arrest at Hansando-do.

4th day of 3rd moon. Imprisoned at Seoul.

1st day of 4th moon. Released under the order to enlist as a soldier under the Field Marshall Kwon Yul.

11th day of 4th moon. His mother passed away.

7th moon. Admiral Won Kyun (who replaced admiral Yi Sun-sin) was defeated by Japanese fleet and beheaded in his refuge.

22nd day of 7th moon. Appointed Supreme Naval Commander.

8th moon. Resumed his duty. All he could gather was 12 ships and 120 sailors.

9th moon. Had a great victory in the campaign at Myongnyang.

10th moon. The third son Myon died in a fight against the Japanese Army at his home, Asan.

1598. 2nd moon. Moved his Navy to Kogum-do.

7th moon, Organized United Naval Forces with the Ming Chinese commodore Chen Lien.

19th day of 11th moon. Died in the final victorious fight against the retreating Japanese.

Bibliography

Yi, Sun-sin, Kim, Kyung-su (translator), *Nanjung Ilgi: War Diary*, Joyful Reading Press, 2004.

Andohi, Kotaro, *History and Theory of Relations of Japan, Korea and China*, Japanese Institute of Korean Studies, 1964.

Ballard, G. A., Vice Admiral, British Royal Navy, *The influence of the Sea on the Political History of Japan*, E. P. Dutton, 1921.

Choi, Doo-hwan, *A Collected Works of Admiral Yi Sun-sin*, Wooseok, 1999.

Ha, Tae-hung, *Nanjung Ilgi: War Diary of Admiral Yi Sun-sin*, Yonsei University Press, 1977.

Ha, Tae-hung, *Imjin Changch'o: Memorials to Court*, Yonsei University Press, 1981.

Hujizka, Akinao, *In Admiration of Admiral Yi Sun-sin*, Kyung Hee Vol. 8, 1977.

Kim, Hoon, *His leadership, A Historic Turning Point*, Soonchunhyang University Press, 2004.

Kim, Su-yong, *Naval Battles of Yi, Nelson, and Togo*, Military Studies, 1997.

Kim, Jung-jin, *Kobukson*, Random House Joongang, 2005.

Roh, Byung-cheon, *To Know Yi Sun-sin is to win the Japanese.* 21c Military Institute, 2005.

Sato Destaro, *A Military History of the Emperor*, Su Moon Sa, 1908.

Published by Korean Spirit & Culture Promotion Project

Korean Spirit & Culture Promotion Project is a 501(c)(3) not for profit organization that was formed under the Diamond Sutra Recitation Group (Chungwoo Buddhist Foundation) in October 2005 to promote Korean history and culture. KSCPP has been publishing and distributing free booklets and DVDs on Korean heritage. Please direct all inquries to kscpp@diamondsutra.org.

New York
158-16 46 Ave., Flushing, NY 11358
☎ 718-539-9108
New Jersey
190 Mountain Rd, Ringoes, NJ 08551
☎ 609-333-9422
Los Angeles
2197 Seaview Dr, Fullerton, CA 92833
☎ 562-644-8949
Atlanta
2100 Bishop Creek Drive, Marietta,
GA 30062 ☎ 770-640-1284

South Korea
131-80 Seongbuk-dong, Seongbuk-gu
Seoul 136-824
☎ 82-2-742-0172
Germany
Hiltistr, 7a 86916 Kaufering
☎ 49-8191-70618
United Kingdom
57 Amberwood Rise, New Malden,
Surrey KT3 5JQ
☎ 44-208-942-1640

* When you finish this booklet, please donate it to a library or school so that it can be shared with others. It would also be greatly appreciated if you could leave your comments and impressions in the guestbook at www.kscpp.net or www.koreanhero.net. Thank you.